CARING for YOUR PARENTS in THEIR SENIOR YEARS

CARING for YOUR PARENTS in THEIR SENIOR YEARS

A Guide for Grown-up Children

WILLIAM MOLLOY, MD

FIREFLY BOOKS

A FIREFLY BOOK

Cataloguing in Publication Data

Molloy, William, 1953–
   Caring for your parents in their senior years

ISBN 1-55209-205-4

1. Aging parents – Care. 2. Parent and adult child. I. Title.

HQ1063.6.M64   1998   362.82   C97-932298-7

First published in Canada in 1996, 1998 by Key Porter Books Limited

Published in the United States in 1998
by Firefly Books (U.S.) Inc.
P.O. Box 1338
Ellicott Station
Buffalo, New York, USA
14205

Printed and bound in Canada

98 99 00 01 6 5 4 3 2 1

*This book is dedicated
to my son, Jim*

Youth is the time for the adventures of the body, but age for the triumphs of the mind.

LOGAN PEARSALL SMITH

Contents

Acknowledgments

I would like to express my deep appreciation to my wife, Deborah, and my son, Alexander; my brothers, Dick, Tom, Frank, John, and Clancy; my sisters, Mary, June, and Sarah; for their love and support while I was writing this.

I am grateful to Laurie Coulter, Ken Kilpatrick, David Schultz, Mav Hall, Dr. John Roy, and Nancy Leslie for all their help and patience with the editing.

I would also like to thank Judy Lever, Andrea Vertesi, Elaine Prinicipi, Lori Pokoradi, Irene Tuttle, David Strang, Rosalie Jubelius, Tim Standish, Rosalie Perovich, Patricia Carter, Stephanie Smith, Sacha Dubois, and Stephen Woeller for their hard work and dedication to our clinic and the Geriatric Research Group.

Introduction

Whoever deeply searches out the truth
And will not be deceived by paths untrue
Shall turn unto himself his inward gaze
Shall bring his wandering thoughts in circle home
And teach his heart that what it seeks abroad
It holds in its own treasure chests within

BOETHIUS, *THE CONSOLATION OF PHILOSOPHY*

My sister Mary called from Ireland at four on a Sunday morning: "Mum had a stroke last night and she's in a coma. They think she's dying. She's asking for you. The only words she spoke were: 'Where's Willie?' I'm sorry, but I don't want you to hear this after she's dead. I feel you should know. Can you come home?"

I felt physically sick, as well as a great emptiness. I had dreaded this call for fourteen years, ever since I had left Ireland. As a geriatrician, I care for patients with dementia, particularly Alzheimer's disease. Sons and daughters come to my clinic worried, exhausted, angry, and burned out because they can't deal with their aging parents. But until I had to deal with my own mother's stroke, aging had never threatened me in such a personal way.

That phone call and the series of events that followed changed me profoundly. I was forced to face some difficult questions head on. What can I do? How can I help? Is it possible to come to terms with this suffering and find meaning from this experience? How do I prepare for, and deal with, my own old age?

Like other people caring for aging parents, I felt squeezed between competing demands from my work, my children, my spouse, my friends, and my parents. How could I cope with them all? I began to understand why some children of aging parents just sat and wept in my office. They felt overwhelmed, shell-shocked, and trapped. They didn't know where to start, and they didn't have a plan. Society, in adolescent denial, had not prepared them for this challenge.

When the call came telling me of my mother's stroke, I was exhausted. I'd just returned from a lecture tour in Australia. It was my son's seventh birthday the next day. There was a stack of mail in my office, and my patients' appointments were backed up for a month. After talking to Mary, I spent hours on the phone trying to work out the logistics of a flight to Ireland. The cheapest fare I could get was an "executive seat" the next day. I didn't have the money. "Oh God, Mum, don't die now," I prayed.

I phoned home again. My father answered. Although he was upset, he was fairly philosophical: "If she's going to get better, she will, and if she's going to die, she will. It's in God's hands now. Only he knows what will happen. She's in a coma. There's nothing you can do. She wouldn't even recognize you now if you came. I'll tell you when to come home. Take care of yourself and your family first."

Later, I talked to other family members and prayed that Mum would hold on until after her grandson's birthday, until after a planned trip to Boston, until I got the money, until I was ready—then it would be okay for her to die. I felt ashamed that I could think about my mother's death in such a selfish, cold fashion.

In a few days, she woke up. Her right side was paralyzed and she couldn't speak, but she could eat. I had a reprieve. I didn't have to go home immediately.

Like all critical stages of development, aging and death provide some interesting challenges. They tend to create victims and survivors. Victims are like children frozen by fear of the boogiemen under their beds. Survivors look under the bed.

The expected loss of my mother forced me to confront my own mortality. I started to experience my own aging in a new way, one that fundamentally changed my perception of myself and my life. I questioned my decisions. Had my life been meaningful? Had my relationships been truthful and worthwhile? Had I lived life according to my principles? Would I "one day" do those things I dreamed about, or would my dreams just fade away, submerged by the reality I had created? Was any of it important at all?

Although I lost a certain youthful innocence in this process, I gained a sense of accomplishment and self-confidence. I turned to sport, literature, and hobbies with a new appreciation. I found a richer sense of pleasure and happiness in my marriage, children, friends, and job. Life felt more fragile, more transient, and more precious because, in a very real sense, my parents' aging was a dress-rehearsal for my own.

My mother and father both died while I was writing this book. I never had the opportunity to talk with them about death and loss, to have the conversation I wished we could have had. I never got to thank them enough or to tell them some of the things I wish I had had a chance to say.

I experienced their deaths in very different ways. When my mother died, I felt tremendous sadness. When my father died, I felt relief. There are no satisfactory good-byes. Death always leaves us with a sense of loss, futility, and sadness. But a parent's aging and death also offer opportunities for us to learn and grow.

This book is for family members who want to help their aging parents. It provides practical information and tools to keep parents safe, healthy, vital, and linked to the world. It will enable sons and daughters to plan for and cope with aging in a healthy and loving fashion. It is my earnest hope that *Caring for Your Parents in Their Senior Years* will be used by children to understand and discuss the important issues they face with their parents in old age. It's a conversation we all desperately need to have, but most children don't know how or where to begin. I hope this book helps you to share love, peace, and wisdom with your parents.

1
Is This Normal?

When elderly parents start to have social, physical, functional, or emotional problems, the first question children ask is, "Is this normal aging or disease?" The second question—"Can it be reversed?"—is just as important.

Unfortunately, many people have such a negative attitude toward aging that they expect to become disabled when they get older. Some parents don't even bother to report their problems, thinking they're an inevitable part of old age. Likewise, some children—even doctors—who see elders failing do nothing, adopting their attitude of, "Well, what do you expect at their age?" Every week I see elders who have had problems for years that could have been improved, or even cured, if they, their children, or their doctors had sought help sooner.

As we age, we become more susceptible to a whole range of diseases. When an older person starts to deteriorate, the challenge is to determine whether the change is the result of a treatable disease or of the aging process.

Common Physical Changes

Hearing Loss

Maurice is a very pleasant 80-year-old who lives alone. Lately he has become withdrawn and confused. His family thinks he is developing Alzheimer's disease. During his appointment with me in the clinic, he couldn't really understand what I was saying and often gave inappropriate answers to my questions. When we tested his hearing, he was practically deaf. Yet he had never complained of hearing loss. In conversations he heard some words and tried to fill in the blanks. He frequently got it wrong, but he refused to wear a hearing aid because he insisted that he didn't need one.

It is estimated that almost half of adults aged 65 or more have some degree of hearing loss. One in three has significant hearing loss. Of those over 80, almost every second person has significant hearing loss. The typical hearing loss associated with aging is "presbycusis," which is loss of hearing in the high-frequency range. Older women complain that their spouses don't listen to them. In fact, their husbands can't hear their high-pitched voices.

Helen Keller said, "Blindness cuts people off from things, deafness cuts people off from people." Hearing loss in older people can lead to isolation, loneliness, and depression. They withdraw from social interactions because they can't hear anything in restaurants, public places, or rooms with background noise. Relatives and friends may also withdraw because trying to have conversations with these individuals is exhausting and frustrating. Children who are not aware of the problem may even think their parent is becoming vague or demented because he or she does not respond appropriately in conversations. It's simply amazing how many times hearing loss is missed and diagnosed as Alzheimer's disease when a hearing aid is all that is needed to fix the problem.

For these reasons, it is important to be aware of the following warning signs of hearing loss: The person

- turns the radio or television volume up very high;
- stops watching television or listening to the radio (especially if his or her spouse or children have complained about the volume);
- wears a blank stare in a conversation and misses essential points;
- often asks you to repeat what you've said;
- turns his or her "good ear" toward you when listening;
- puts a hand to his or her ear in a conversation, or moves toward you to hear better.

Like Maurice, some older adults deny they have a problem with their hearing. When family members insist there is a problem, the elder complains that they are exaggerating or interfering. If you find that your parent becomes defensive when you bring up this topic, it may be wise to refer the problem to a doctor and let her handle it. Parents are more likely to believe a doctor than a child or spouse.

Dr. Richard Crilly, a geriatrician friend of mine, tells a story that illustrates this problem. He was examining an older woman who was quite deaf. He struggled through a long, exhausting history and examination, shouting at the top of his lungs to make himself heard. Finally, tired of yelling, he told her she had a bad hearing problem and should get a hearing aid. "Oh, I did, Doctor. I have it in my bag," she replied. Richard lifted up her bag and shouted into it, "Can you hear better if I speak in here?"

Hearing aids If hearing loss is suspected, a hearing assessment can be arranged through your parent's family doctor. During the assessment, the patient wears headphones. Sounds at different frequencies are transmitted to each ear to measure the loss on each side so that the most appropriate aid can be prescribed for each ear.

There are many different types of hearing aids. One, worn on the chest, has a microphone, an amplifier, a receiver, and a battery. However, it picks up scratchy noises from clothing as it is jostled about. The most common type is the "behind-the-ear aid." Its very small volume controls and on/off switch require a lot of manual dexterity, which is a problem for many older adults. The controls of another type are incorporated into the arm of a pair of glasses.

A wide variety of devices are available for the hearing impaired. They include lights on telephones or doorbells, and amplifiers on the telephone, radio, or television.

Tips for communicating You should encourage your parent to wear an aid and keep it serviced, and to ask for clarification if he or she doesn't hear very well. Choose a quiet location to have a conversation. Your parent may want to switch off the radio or television while you are talking together. Speak slowly and clearly and leave lots of time for your mother or father to ask questions. Use a notebook if necessary to clarify a point.

For further information, contact the National Information Center at Gallaudet University. Phone: (202) 651-5051.

Failing Eyesight

Our eyesight deteriorates as we age. Fortunately, wearing glasses does not seem to carry the stigma that wearing a hearing aid seems to, possibly because many people begin wearing glasses at an early age. As with hearing loss, if you find that your parent becomes defensive when you bring up the subject of failing eyesight, it may be wise to refer the problem to a doctor. Making improvements in your parent's home environment (see Chapter 5) can also be helpful.

Severe loss of vision, leading to blindness, is one of the most feared disabilities of old age. The damage to the delicate tissues of the eye, which has a wide variety of causes, tends to be cumulative over the course of a lifetime. The prevalence of blindness in the elderly is almost one hundred times greater than among children. In developed countries, the common causes of blindness in older people are cataracts, glaucoma, and retinal disease from macular degeneration or diabetes. All of these conditions increase in frequency with advancing age.

Glaucoma Glaucoma is caused by damage to the optic nerve from increased pressure within the eye. Fluid is produced in the eye and circulates through different chambers. In glaucoma, there is a problem with the filtering system, and fluid becomes trapped in one of the two chambers of the eye. This fluid buildup causes increased pressure within the eye and damages the optic nerve. Visual impairment is slow and progressive. It is very difficult to diagnose this damage, especially in the early stages, because the initial damage occurs in the peripheral vision on the far-outside fields of vision. This loss is rarely noticeable, except by formal testing.

The goal of treatment is to prevent further damage to the eye by lowering the pressure within it. Topical medications (eye drops) or pills are used to lower the pressure to a level that is tolerated by the optic nerve. If this treatment is unsuccessful, laser surgery can be used to burn a hole in the filtering system, thereby allowing the fluid to circulate.

Occasionally the meshwork filter between the chambers can become blocked, causing the pressure within the eye to rise suddenly. This can cause severe pain, blurring of vision, colored halos around lights, and nausea and vomiting. Eye drops, oral medications, and laser surgery are used to relieve the obstruction and allow passage of the fluid between the different chambers.

Cataracts The crystalline lens of the eye is a unique structure in the body. Its cells do not divide and are the same ones that were formed in the uterus. As the lens ages, it becomes more rigid and has increasing difficulty distinguishing between distant and near objects. Older people notice that they have difficulty reading and require bifocals and reading glasses. The lens responds to any damage by losing clarity and forming a cataract.

The treatment of cataracts is generally surgical. An incision is made in the eye, and the entire lens is removed and replaced with a plastic lens. The improvement in vision after surgery is often dramatic.

Macular degeneration This common cause of impaired vision affects central vision but rarely causes total blindness. The inner lining of the eye, the retina, degenerates, resulting in gradual loss of vision. Since the peripheral vision is usually spared, the person retains enough sight to perform basic functions, for example, to walk independently. In certain cases laser treatment may be helpful.

Falls

Helen, a 78-year-old, had a slight stroke last year which left her with mild arm weakness. She also has cataracts, high blood pressure, and osteoarthritis. Helen takes blood pressure pills, aspirin, and sleeping pills. She had bunion surgery ten years ago and fell two years ago without injury when she slipped on some ice. Now she is in hospital after falling in her house and breaking her hip.

People of all ages trip and fall from time to time, perhaps slipping on ice or running up the stairs too fast; but falls are more common as we get older. About a third of people over 65, living in their own homes, fall every year, and this percentage rises among people living in nursing homes. Falls tend to be more serious for older people. About 10 percent of them result in a significant injury. One in twenty causes a fracture such as a broken hip or wrist. After falling and injuring themselves, many people become afraid of doing it again and limit their activities, and thus their enjoyment of life.

For the purpose of this discussion, it is not considered a fall if a parent is knocked over in the street, catches a bicycle wheel in a sewer grate, or faints or has a seizure. The type of fall discussed here is one in which your parent's legs just give out, or he or she trips over an uneven surface and can't regain balance to prevent falling. These types of falls usually don't happen to healthy younger people.

What causes these falls? It's almost always a combination of many different things. Helen, for example, has cataracts, which may prevent her from seeing obstacles; arthritis, which may reduce her ability to exercise and keep up her muscle strength; and high blood pressure, which requires treatment that may make her light-headed. The bunion surgery has made her feet less flexible and has reduced sensation, and the stroke may have caused muscle weakness and poor balance. Taking sleeping pills may slow her down and affect her balance. Any one of these factors alone would not make her fall, but together they might. In general, older people have slower reflexes, less muscle strength, and reduced balance. A minor stumble in a younger person turns into a major fall for an older person with these problems.

Although there is usually no single "cure," you can decrease the risk of your parent's falling. In Helen's case, the family doctor should be asked to review the medications to see if any increase the risk of falls and can be stopped or changed. Helen also needs to keep active by walking, cycling, or swimming to increase her muscle strength and balance. A doctor or physiotherapist can prescribe an activity program. A podiatrist or chiropodist can examine her feet and advise about shoes with proper supports. Slip-ons, open heels, and shoes with slippery soles should be avoided. Other measures to take include correcting poor lighting, removing or securing loose throw rugs, removing clutter, and covering slippery floors. An occupational therapist can come to the home to suggest modifications to the house or apartment to make it safer, and to teach her safer ways to move about (see Chapter 5). Finally, Helen's vision should be checked regularly.

Falls can be a frightening prospect for older adults; nobody wants to end up with a broken hip. Fortunately, most falls can be prevented.

Foot Problems

Foot problems are common in older adults. Most can be prevented by wearing proper footwear. Often people don't realize that their feet grow larger as they age. Almost 90 percent of foot problems in women are caused by too-tight shoes. Suitable footwear, cutting nails properly (they should be cut straight across), and early attention to symptoms will prevent the majority of foot problems.

Constipation

Normal bowel activity leads to the passage of stool between three times daily and three times weekly. Between 60 and 80 percent of a normal stool is made up of water. An increase in the water content occurs with diarrhea, and a decrease results in harder stool or constipation. Constipation is a common problem of old age, most likely caused by a low-fiber diet, inactivity, reduced fluid intake, and ignoring the call to defecate. Most people with natural bowel activity feel the need to defecate in the early morning, after breakfast. This is called the "gastrocolic reflex." Ignoring it suppresses the reflex and leads to rectal filling. There are also medical conditions and drugs that worsen constipation.

Many older people have motility problems in their bowel from the chronic use of laxatives. There may be more people addicted to laxatives worldwide than to any other drugs. Some believe a daily bowel movement is essential to health and vitality. This may lead to the regular use of purgatives, such as liquid paraffin, senna, and phenolphthalein. Long-standing use of these types of laxatives damages the bowel and leaves it flaccid and unable to evacuate without stimulation. This is called a "cathartic bowel."

The best treatment for constipation is to prevent it by following three simple rules: Eat a diet containing adequate roughage, drink enough fluids, and keep active. If your parent has a problem with constipation, it is essential that he or she avoid the regular use of laxatives and try to maintain a regular bowel habit naturally.

Incontinence

Agnes is a very pleasant 86-year-old. When I examined her, she had a pad in her panties. Asked why she used it, she said she was afraid she would not make it to the bathroom in time. A few months previously, she had wet herself in a restaurant. She stopped going out after that because she was terrified it would happen again. When I asked Agnes if she had sought help for the problem, she replied, "But don't people normally lose control of their water when they grow old?"

Although incontinence is more common as we age, it is *not* a normal part of aging. The majority of people with incontinence can be cured or helped with proper treatment.

Incontinence is any involuntary loss of urine. Between 5 and 25 percent of people suffer from it, including about a third of those in hospital and half of those living in institutions. Women are twice as likely to develop it as men.

This disease is undertreated and underdiagnosed because people fail to tell their doctors about it, and doctors often ignore patients when they do tell them they have incontinence. People hide it because they are ashamed. In almost half of the cases, the family is not even aware of it. Their parents use pads and go to the bathroom frequently. If incontinence remains untreated, it not only can cause skin rashes, pressure sores, and urinary tract infections, but also can limit the person's activities. Like Agnes, older adults with this problem may lose confidence and stay in their homes because they are afraid of wetting themselves.

Incontinence can lead to depression, withdrawal, sexual dysfunction, and anxiety. There are many effective treatments available, and usually it can be helped, or even cured. But first it is necessary to find out what is causing it.

Incontinence may be caused by drugs, infections, or problems with muscles at the outlet from the bladder. Approximately 5 percent of women taking blood-pressure medications (alpha-blocker medications) develop incontinence as a side effect. If they are not aware of this, they can endure an unnecessary side effect that can ruin their self-respect and quality of life. Other medications may also cause or worsen incontinence. Sleeping pills and other sedatives, especially when taken by older people, may relax the muscles in the bladder and cause incontinence. Water pills (diuretics) cause brisk urination, which aggravates urgency and urge incontinence. Some over-the-counter medications, such as antihistamines, can block emptying and lead to overflow incontinence.

This problem should always be reported to a doctor. Something as simple as a bladder infection may be the culprit and it may be cleared up with antibiotics.

Stress incontinence In this case, urine leakage is provoked by an increase in pressure in the abdomen. It is usually caused by coughing, sneezing, laughing, or jumping. Women are more often affected than men. Most people with stress incontinence have a very mobile bladder neck and urethra (the tube that carries urine from the bladder). They also have weak pelvic-floor muscles, causing the bladder to descend under stress. The abdominal pressure induced by a cough or a sneeze is transmitted to the bladder, but not to the urethra in its low position. Pressure on the bladder increases and is not matched by any closing pressure in the urethra to prevent leakage.

Special exercises (Kegel exercises) to strengthen the pelvic muscles can cure the problem. To do Kegel exercises:

- Contract the muscles in the pelvic floor (it should feel like you are pulling up everything inside your pelvic region) and hold.
- Count one second, two seconds, three, until unable to hold any longer. Rest for five to ten seconds, then try again. With practice, you should be able to contract the muscles for ten seconds.
- Perform a set of ten exercises once each waking hour.
- After five to six weeks, improvement should be evident if the exercise has been faithfully done *and* there is not another cause of urinary loss.
- Once control has been reestablished, the exercise may be reduced to once every other day.

Surgery to the bladder neck and urethra to push them back into the pelvis usually cures stress incontinence. Sometimes drug treatment also helps.

In men, this type of incontinence is usually the result of injury to the sphincter during transurethral resection of the prostate (TURP) or radical prostatectomy (removal of the prostate). The incidence of incontinence following radical prostatectomy ranges from 3 to 10 percent of patients. People who have suffered an injury (pelvic fracture, spinal injury) may also develop this type of incontinence.

Urge incontinence This is involuntary urine loss associated with a strong and sudden desire to void. In these cases, people feel an overwhelming urge to urinate and have to rush to the toilet as quickly as possible. If they don't make it in time, they lose urine.

Normally, as the bladder fills, the bladder contractions intensify gradually, as does the urge to void. The muscle in the bladder that contracts to empty the bladder is called the "detrusor muscle." In some people, this muscle is unstable and can produce sudden strong contractions with very little warning. Detrusor instability is the most common form of incontinence. It occurs more often in women, and usually has no known cause.

Detrusor instability in men is often associated with bladder-outlet obstruction caused by an enlarged prostate gland or bladder-neck problems. Whether the detrusor muscle itself constitutes the primary trigger for the contraction, or whether it is caused by damage to the nerves that make the muscle contract, remains uncertain. Certain drugs can relieve this problem in both men and women.

Shortness of Breath

Dyspnea, or shortness of breath, is one of the most common disabilities reported by older people. Up to 30 percent of older adults aged between 65 and 75 complain of shortness of breath with activity. More than 35 percent aged 75 or more notice they are short of breath with exertion. Sudden acute dyspnea is a very distressing complaint because the victim thinks he or she is going to suffocate.

Normally a person's breathing rate increases with activity. Healthy adults feel short of breath when their rate of breathing is doubled. The sensation occurs when the breathing rate increases in response to stimulation from the respiratory center in the brain. In unhealthy individuals, the breathing rate can increase with less and less activity, so that eventually the breathing rate increases even at rest, and the person experiences shortness of breath with minimal or no activity.

In old age, the chest wall becomes stiffer and the lungs become less compliant. The lung reserves that provide oxygen during activity diminish, and shortness of breath in response to activity becomes exaggerated. Shortness of breath is a normal accompaniment to old age. However, there are also illnesses that can cause this problem in older people. These include lung diseases such as pneumonia, bronchitis, and asthma. Heart disease can also lead to shortness of breath, as can a wide variety of diseases having to do with the kidneys, liver, blood, brain, or even bone. In addition, many drugs can cause or worsen shortness of breath.

If your parent is experiencing shortness of breath, it is important to arrange a proper checkup by a physician. In the majority of cases, dyspnea can be improved with treatment.

Sexuality

Sam and Veronica had been married for fifty-five years. I was seeing Sam because he had fallen at home. He was taking blood pressure pills that caused his blood pressure to fall when he stood up. I told Sam that I wanted to change his medication, but first I wanted to see if he needed the pills at all. I planned to stop them and see what happened. I mentioned that the pills not only caused blood pressure to fall on standing, but also caused impotence. Veronica shook her head and smiled: "Oh, Doctor, at our age we haven't had any of that for years." I asked Sam when he had started taking the blood pressure pills and it turned out that his impotence began at that time. Pointing out the connection got their attention.

We stopped the pills, and the next time I saw Sam and Veronica they were both very happy indeed. Veronica told me that Sam wanted to stay off the pills no matter what his blood pressure readings were. When he lost weight and cut down on his salt intake, his blood pressure returned to normal. His impotence disappeared. I receive a card from them every Christmas.

Like many people, Sam and Veronica thought impotence was normal in old age. The sexual revolution of the 1960s did little for seniors. There are still barriers in the media, educational systems, religious institutions, and personal morality to the expression of sexuality by the elderly. Despite these barriers, older men and women remain interested and capable of sexual arousal and function. Some studies suggest that physical activity and active sexuality contribute to longevity. Older adults may not engage in vigorous sex, but by all accounts they enjoy sex more because they find it even more intimate and enjoyable than younger adults do.

With advancing age there is a decline in sexual function when the frequency of intercourse is the only factor considered. This decline is usually attributed to the male. When a full range of sexual activity is practiced, not just intercourse, sexual functioning can be maintained, or even increased, in old age. Even in the very old, aged between 80 and 100, 80 percent of men and more than 60 percent of women fantasize or daydream about sex often or very often. Older women have a greater level of sexual interest and activity than do older men. More than 70 percent of men and more than 60 percent of women continue to self-pleasure, and more than 60 percent of men continue to have sexual intercourse. Sexual activity is more frequent in the elderly who live in cultures where sexuality in seniors is accepted and expected.

Normal aging and sexuality In both sexes, the intensity and speed of sexual response decline with advancing age. This change may be caused by a fall in the level of sex hormones. Older people who are unaware of these changes may interpret them as a loss of sexual function. This can lead to fear or anxiety-induced sexual dysfunction (performance anxiety). Men's testosterone levels are highest in the morning or early afternoon, so this may be the best time for sex. Because older men require more manual stimulation to become aroused, they may need to rub themselves against their partners, or their partners may need to stimulate their genitals manually.

Older adults also need to focus on the greater pleasure package rather than just intercourse performance alone. Sex in later life can be more rewarding because the partners are not as rushed or trying as hard to prove themselves. This is the time to explore a variety of ways to experience sexuality and intimacy.

Men, however, are particularly at risk of developing widower's syndrome. When a widower has had a good sex life in the past and has not adequately completed the grieving process before he becomes involved in a new relationship, he may experience good erections with caressing, but lose his erection when he tries to have intercourse. With education and supportive psychotherapy to resolve his grieving, he can reestablish confidence and have a successful sexual relationship.

In women, sexual interest and ability are not dependent on the hormone estrogen, which decreases after menopause. In fact, some women may experience an increase in sexual interest and activity after menopause. The most common problem among older women is dyspareunia (pain during intercourse). Lack of estrogen causes the vagina to shrink, the lining to thin, and the amount of lubrication to decrease during arousal. Women who do not receive hormone replacement therapy can have pain when they pass urine for a few days after intercourse. This lack of lubrication can also cause inflammation and chronic pain, which is persistent throughout the day, regardless of whether intercourse has taken place.

The use of lubricant jelly, such as K-Y, or estrogen treatment allows postmenopausal women to continue to enjoy intercourse with their partners. Many women give up sex because they lack the proper information and are ashamed or embarrassed to ask. Older women also benefit from the use of vibrators to arouse them or bring them to orgasm.

Probably the greatest challenge faced by older women is the lack of partners. Those who are not comfortable with masturbation or same-sex partners cannot experience satisfying sexual relationships because there are not enough available healthy men.

Accepting our parents' sexuality Society needs to recognize and accept the sexual needs of older adults. Children, in particular, often have a problem when a widowed or divorced parent remarries. They do not acknowledge the parent's need for intimacy and companionship. We need to acknowledge that it's normal for older adults to fall in love, start a relationship, and have sex.

Sexuality contributes to self-esteem, well-being, and physical health. The majority of healthy men and women remain interested and active sexually if provided with the opportunity, even in extreme old age. Even those who lose the ability to have intercourse can have a very satisfactory sex life using alternative techniques.

Health Problems after 65

Alzheimer's Disease

Jake, a healthy 64-year-old retired civil servant, had a nice home, a cottage, a boat, and a loving wife and family. He had worked hard and was looking forward to his retirement. Although he didn't smoke or drink and was in great shape physically, he started to forget names, repeat himself, and become mixed up when he went to the store. He got lost driving his car and made mistakes scoring his golf game. The memory loss progressed, and within three years he needed help dressing and grooming. Two years later he wore a diaper, and his family had to put him in a nursing home. He had Alzheimer's disease.

In the developed world, about 2 to 4 percent of all adults, 5 to 10 percent of those aged 65 or more, and about 45 percent of those aged 85 or more suffer from dementia. Dementia causes memory loss of such severity that it interferes with the person's ability to function independently. Of the many causes of dementia, the most common is Alzheimer's disease. Strokes, Parkinson's disease, and head injuries can also cause it.

At first, people with Alzheimer's experience short-term memory loss and repeat themselves because they cannot lay down new information in their brains. After two or three years, more distant memory becomes affected and they may become confused and forget where they live or the names of family members. Decision making becomes a problem, and they have trouble with phones, driving, shopping, or managing finances. They experience difficulty making their wishes known or expressing their thoughts. Many don't even realize they have memory problems.

People with Alzheimer's may also experience dramatic changes in social behavior. They can become frustrated, withdrawn, anxious, angry, aggressive, or depressed. They are afraid to be left alone, refuse help, and believe there are strangers in the house or that people are stealing from them. When they look in the mirror, they see a stranger looking back at them. They are difficult to manage because their behavior changes so often and is so unpredictable. Sleep disturbances cause them to leave their beds at night. They don't recognize their own spouses and may try to throw them out of the house.

In the final stages, Alzheimer's patients lose muscle strength and become bed bound. They lose control of their bowels and bladder and have to wear diapers. In the end, they lose the ability to swallow, and inhale fluid into the lungs and die from pneumonia.

Alzheimer's is not part of normal aging but is a disease process that afflicts predominantly older people. It usually lasts between seven and fourteen years. In first-world countries, Alzheimer's is the single greatest public-health hazard facing society. It's estimated that the 1993 cost of Alzheimer's was $80 billion in the United States. About 10 million people in the United States and the European Union have the disease.

The cause of Alzheimer's disease is not known, and no treatment to slow or arrest the process has been discovered. Certain genes have been associated with the disease. People with the BCHE-K gene are 30 times more likely to develop Alzheimer's than those who do not have it. As the population ages and dementia becomes more common, more people are looking for treatments, and public pressure for a "cure" is mounting. This search for a cure for dementia has become linked with the search for a "cure" or treatment to slow the aging process itself.

For further information on caring for parents with Alzheimer's, see page 156, or contact the Alzheimer's Association, 919 N. Michigan Avenue, Ste. 100, Chicago, IL. Toll-free: 1-800-272-3700; phone: (312) 335-5731.

Arthritis

Joint or muscle pain may be the most common complaint in people aged 65 or more. Almost half of older adults report that arthritis is a problem. However, many aches and pains are not necessarily caused by arthritis. The pain may be the result of muscle sprains, bursitis, tendinitis, or viral illnesses. Nevertheless, up to 90 percent of older men and women show evidence of arthritis on x-rays. Pain and stiffness are usually confined to affected joints, are worse at the end of the day, and are relieved by rest.

In the management of arthritis, it is essential for your parent to understand how to protect his or her joints and remain active at the same time. Proper shoes should be worn and activities should be limited to those that do not unduly stress or damage the joints. Acetaminophen (Tylenol) is useful to manage pain. If it is not effective, aspirin or nonsteroidal anti-inflammatory drugs should be used.

For further information, contact the Arthritis Foundation, P.O. Box 7669, Atlanta, GA 30357-0669. Toll-free: 1-800-283-7800; phone: (404) 872-7100.

Diabetes

Maria is an 84-year-old widow who lives alone. She has become more vague and confused over the past few weeks, is losing weight, and has stopped reading and watching television. She seems to have no energy and has been falling. Her daughter finally persuaded her to visit her doctor. Maria was found to be diabetic. With treatment, her health has improved dramatically.

Diabetes affects people of all ages. It is estimated that about 5 percent of the population and 10 percent of people aged 65 or older have this disease. Twenty percent of people who are overweight are diabetic. Diabetes is a silent and deadly disease because almost half of those with the disease don't even know they have it. Many of those who do know they have it don't adjust their diets and lifestyle to minimize the risks they face. Others don't understand the different treatments they receive and why they take them.

In older adults diabetes can cause confusion, weight loss, and loss of energy. People with diabetes mellitus, "sweet urine disease," can't process glucose (sugar) because their bodies lack insulin or are unable to use it properly. Glucose is the fuel used to produce energy in the body. If cells are deprived of glucose, they can't work properly, and the person runs out of energy and becomes ill.

Common symptoms of diabetes are thirst, dry and flushed skin, and fatigue. Since the body can't use glucose, it builds up in the blood and spills into the urine. It drags water with it and causes water loss from the body. In older adults, diabetes comes on slowly and may damage the heart, eyes, brain, or kidneys, even before the sufferer is diagnosed. It can also affect the nerves and blood vessels in the feet, causing numbness, tingling pain, or poor circulation.

Diabetes is easy to diagnose by measuring the level of sugar in the blood. Treatment involves special diets, drugs, or insulin injections.

Two types of diabetes There are two types of diabetes. Although the treatment of the two is different, both can cause the same long-term health problems.

Type I is juvenile-type diabetes in children. The cells in the pancreas are damaged by a virus and the pancreas suddenly stops making insulin. This type of diabetes is called "insulin-dependent diabetes." People with this type account for about 10 percent of all diabetics. They need insulin every day and must watch their diets carefully. Insulin is not a cure, merely a treatment to control the disease.

Type II is the adult form of diabetes. This type usually affects adults aged 40 or more. With aging, there is a tendency to reduce activity levels without reducing food intake. As a result, body weight increases. When it rises more than 20 percent over ideal body weight, the person is at risk of developing diabetes. Eighty percent of adults who develop the disease are overweight. The other risk factors are family history, age, and stress.

With this type, the pancreas continues to produce insulin, but the insulin does not work properly. It fails to limit the level of blood glucose or properly activate the cells to take in glucose. Because most people with this type of diabetes do not need insulin injections, it is known as "non-insulin-dependent diabetes." This is the common form of diabetes among older people and accounts for more than 85 percent of cases in the elderly.

Type II, which may take several years to develop, can often be controlled with diet and exercise, although some people also need medications.

Complications The presence of these factors increases the risk of developing complications from diabetes:

- Poor control of blood glucose through diet, exercise, or medication. Good control can prevent or delay most serious complications.
- High blood cholesterol and fat levels cause hardening of the arteries (arteriosclerosis). If the blood cholesterol levels are high, special changes in the diet may help. High blood pressure damages the arteries. Blood pressure checks are recommended at least once a year.
- Cigarette smoking damages the lungs, increases the risk of cancer, and also damages the arteries. People with diabetes should not smoke.

Since many complications of diabetes have early warning signs, quick treatment can prevent further damage. The best protection for people with this disease is to be aware of the early signs of diabetes and have regular checkups.

Diabetes and the eyes Diabetes can cause blindness, but most diabetics do not become blind. Good control of blood sugars and blood pressure can prevent it.

Your diabetic parent should have an eye examination at least once a year by an eye specialist so that, if there is a problem, treatment can be given early to prevent long-term side effects. Diabetes can damage the retina. The most common treatment for a retina damaged by diabetes is called "photocoagulation." A finely focused laser beam of light is used to destroy small vessels in the retina that might break and bleed into the eye. This procedure can also be used to repair retinal detachment.

If your diabetic parent notices any change in his or her vision, the doctor should be contacted immediately.

Diabetes and the kidneys The kidneys contain filters known as "glomeruli," which remove waste from the blood while preventing the loss of important substances. Diabetes damages the tiny blood vessels in the glomeruli. Proteins then leak through the filters and can be found in the urine. To detect this problem, diabetics should have their urine tested yearly.

If the kidneys are seriously damaged, the body will retain fluid, and the feet, hands, and eyelids will swell. If the kidneys fail, waste products can be artificially removed by hemodialysis (filtering the blood with a kidney machine) or peritoneal dialysis (filtering the blood by injecting fluid into the abdomen). Severely damaged kidneys can be replaced with kidney transplants. New drugs, which have been developed to prevent the body from rejecting the donor kidney, make this procedure safer and much more successful.

Risk factors for kidney damage in diabetics include poor control of the disease, high blood pressure, kidney infections, or exposure to a particular type of x-ray that damages the kidneys.

Diabetes and the nervous system Damage to nerves (neuropathy) is a common complication of diabetes. Nerves are damaged by high levels of blood glucose and poor nourishment when the small blood vessels supplying them are destroyed. The nerves in the arms and legs (peripheral nerves) or the nerves to the heart and other organs (autonomic nerves) are commonly affected. The first signs of damage to nerves in the limbs is numbness, pain, or a burning sensation in the hands and feet. Later, there is loss of ability to feel touch, pain, or heat. Injuries to the skin may be ignored or go unnoticed by diabetics with nerve damage. This is particularly dangerous in the feet, where the circulation can be compromised by damage to blood vessels. Infection can lead to gangrene. Proper foot care is essential for diabetics.

When the nerves to certain organs are damaged, the heart may race, stomach emptying may be delayed, the bladder may not empty, men may experience problems during sexual activity (impotence), blood pressure may fall on standing (postural hypotension), or diarrhea may occur. A wide variety of treatments is available for these problems.

Diabetes and large blood vessels In diabetics, fat may be deposited on the walls of large blood vessels, causing narrowing. This reduces blood flow and can lead to heart attacks (myocardial infarction), strokes (cerebral infarction), or gangrene in the feet.

Treatment Diabetics should first and foremost educate themselves about the disease and then take responsibility for it. Diabetes is not the end of the world; millions live with it every day. Here are some general guidelines to share with your diabetic parent:

- Monitor your own disease and keep control.
- Follow your meal plan and eat a high-roughage diet.
- Avoid foods high in animal fat and cholesterol.
- Get regular exercise.
- Do not smoke.
- Have your blood pressure, eyes, and urine checked at least once a year.
- Examine your feet regularly and learn how to care for them, or see a podiatrist regularly. If there are abrasions, broken skin, ulcers, or any sign of infection, get attention immediately. Prompt attention can prevent complications of diabetes and promote a long and healthy life.

For further information, contact the American Diabetes Association, 1660 Duke Street, P.O. Box 25757, Alexandria, VA 22314. Phone: (703) 549-1500.

Osteoporosis

Jane was bending over to pick up a shopping bag. She suddenly felt a sharp pain in her back, at the bottom of her rib cage. At first she thought she had pulled a muscle. In fact, she had fractured a vertebra in her backbone.

Our bones give us form and allow us to stand upright and move around. They protect our organs and store calcium, a vital mineral. Bones are living organs made of cells, protein, and minerals. They grow throughout life and reach their greatest density in middle age, decreasing from then on into old age. New bone is constantly being made as old bone is broken down and absorbed into the body. This whole process is delicately balanced. In osteoporosis, a bone disease affecting older people, the loss of bone is greater than the formation of new bone.

The bones of people with osteoporosis become thin and brittle, are unable to bear heavy loads, and break easily. Normal activities such as carrying groceries, bending over, coughing, or sneezing can fracture bones. This disease can also cause vertebrae to collapse, resulting in loss of height and increased curvature of the spine (kyphosis).

Osteoporosis can lead to serious disability, and even death. It strikes silently. The first symptom, back pain, often doesn't occur until the disease is well advanced. Osteoporosis does not appear on x-rays until as much as 30 percent of bone density has been lost. It is during the early stages of the disease that bone loss can be prevented or minimized. By taking precautions, it is possible to reduce significantly the chances of developing the condition. However, with proper care, people who have it can lead active and productive lives.

Risk factors for osteoporosis Osteoporosis occurs in men and women, but it is much more common in women over age 50. Several million American women suffer from the disease, and many millions more are at risk of developing it. About 20 percent of men aged 70 or more have osteoporosis.

The major risk factors are female gender and advanced age. This risk is mainly linked to estrogen deficiency, which occurs after menopause. Almost 25 percent of post-menopausal women develop the condition, and this increases to a staggering 50 percent of women aged 70 or over. Women who lack estrogen because of early menopause or premature menopause from surgey are at increased risk of developing osteoporosis earlier than the general population. Those with a family history of the disease are also at increased risk. Blacks are less likely than Eurasians or Caucasians to develop the condition. People who have light frames or smaller physiques, or who lack calcium in their diets, are more likely to develop it. Lack of regular physical activity increases the risk, as does taking cortisone, smoking, or excessive use of alcohol or caffeine. Although these risk factors indicate which groups of people are more likely to get osteoporosis, we can't say for certain which individuals in these groups will get the disease.

Preventing osteoporosis Osteoporosis does not cause any symptoms. The pain, disability, and deformity which characterize the disease are the result of fractures. By the time fractures begin, the condition may be well advanced and almost half of the bone density lost. At this stage the disease is harder to treat because it is very difficult to increase the density of bones. It is much easier to prevent loss of bone density than to replace it once it has been lost.

Eating proper amounts of calcium helps maintain bone density. Dairy products like cheese, yogurt, and ice cream are rich in calcium. They contribute about 75 percent of the calcium in the average North American diet. Canned sardines and salmon, with the bones, are good sources. Broccoli and other leafy green vegetables also contain calcium, although much smaller amounts.

If your parent is allergic to milk and milk products, a wide variety of specially formulated foods containing calcium can be substituted. Those who are watching their calories can buy low-fat milk products made from skim, 1 or 2 percent milk.

A variety of calcium supplements are available. Each contains a certain amount of elemental calcium or pure calcium. Calcium carbonate has 40 percent pure calcium; however, calcium gluconate has only 10 percent. Obviously it's better to take the former. Certain antacids such as Tums are a good source of calcium. Multivitamins with minerals also contain it.

Regular exercise plays an important role in preventing osteoporosis. The more stress the bones receive, the stronger they become. The worst thing we can do for our bones is to take to our beds and rest. Any weight-bearing activity, such as walking, tennis, dancing, golfing, skiing, or skating, is good for bones.

Estrogen replacement Estrogen levels decline after menopause or after surgical removal of the ovaries. Levels can be raised, however, using hormone replacement therapy (HRT). This is effective in preventing bone loss and reduces the risk of osteoporosis. HRT also reduces the risk of heart disease and treats other symptoms of menopause—hot flashes, vaginal dryness, and sleep disturbance—as well as preventing memory loss.

Women are unable to take estrogen if they have a history of liver problems or vaginal bleeding, or are at high risk for breast cancer. There may be an increase in the risk of breast cancer associated with the use of HRT. In making the decision to start HRT, the wish to lessen symptoms and to reduce the risk of osteoporosis and heart disease is weighed against the potential increased risk of cancer.

Women with osteoporosis who cannot or do not want to take HRT may be treated with etidronate (Didronel, Didrocol) or alendronate (Fosamax). These drugs act directly on bone to stop breakdown, thus effectively maintaining bone mass. They are also the treatment of choice for men with the disease.

If you are concerned about your mother's risk of developing osteoporosis, discuss it with her and your family doctor, and perhaps see a specialist. Advise your mother to eat well, to make sure she gets enough calcium, to stay active, and to avoid medications such as cortisone that increase the risk of osteoporosis. The recommended calcium intake for older adults is about 800 milligrams every day. Those who have osteoporosis may require more. Advise your mother to consult her doctor or dietician for advice.

For further information, contact the National Osteoporosis Foundation at 1-800-223-9994.

Parkinson's Disease

Seymour was an active 75-year-old. He noticed that his voice was becoming faint and that he had started to slow down considerably. He developed a shake in his right hand and began to stumble. When I first saw him, it was obvious that he had Parkinson's disease. I prescribed an activity program and dopamine, and his symptoms improved dramatically.

The terms "Parkinson's disease," "Parkinson syndrome," and "Parkinsonism" are often used interchangeably for a chronic brain disease which causes tremor, slow movements, and muscle stiffness. An area of the brain called "the substantia nigra" contains cells which produce a chemical called "dopamine." With the death of these cells, and the resulting deficiency of dopamine, the transmission of messages between the body's nerve cells is blocked, making movement difficult.

Parkinson's is more common after age 55, but it can occur in younger people. Men and women are equally affected.

Today, in North America, almost 700,000 people have Parkinson's disease, and more than half of them were diagnosed before reaching retirement age. This condition is not thought to be inherited. Research studies are in progress to determine possible causes when it affects more than one family member.

Symptoms include:

- tremor of the limbs when at rest;
- muscular rigidity;
- slowness of movement;
- difficulty with balance and walking;
- reduced volume and clarity of speech;
- difficulty with fine movements (for example, handwriting).

Neurologists diagnose Parkinson's disease by going over the patient's medical history and by careful clinical examination. Often tests are done to rule out other conditions which may resemble Parkinson's, but there are no x-rays or tests that can confirm the diagnosis.

Treatment Treatment is needed to correct the person's chemical imbalance and allow him or her to function better. Drugs alleviate the symptoms but do not halt the progression of the disease. As symptoms progress, more medication is needed. Ongoing research is focused on finding more effective treatments.

Rehabilitation therapy is aimed at promoting independence and improving all aspects of functional ability, and includes the following approaches:

- assessment of mobility, balance, and posture, and prescription of a specific exercise program;
- analysis of walking problems and help to correct or minimize difficulties;
- instruction in the use of adaptive equipment (walkers or canes);

- promotion of safety awareness;
- training in more efficient ways to perform tasks, in order to conserve energy;
- instruction in techniques for stress management.

Speech therapy evaluates speech problems and develops programs to meet individual needs.

For further information, contact the National Parkinson Foundation, 1501 N.W. Ninth Avenue, Miami, FLA 331360. Toll-free: 1-800-327-4545.

Strokes

Theresa had a stroke three months ago. Now she has weakness in her right side and difficulty expressing herself. She bumps into things, cries a lot, and has trouble eating. Nothing her family does seems to please her. The family is frustrated because the emotional aftereffects of the stroke seem out of proportion to the physical changes.

Families often have more difficulty dealing with the mental and emotional changes from a stroke than they do dealing with the physical problems. Strokes (cerebrovascular accidents) are caused by damage to the brain when an artery is blocked by clots or hemorrhage and cannot supply the brain with oxygen. The person suffers the most disability immediately after the stroke, and then begins to recover. Recovery can continue for up to six months. In fact, most of the recovery occurs in the first few weeks. Any significant recovery is unlikely to occur after six months.

Different types of strokes affect different parts of the brain and, for this reason, each person's disability is unique. Some areas may function normally, while others may not. The affected person may be able to do some tasks but be completely unable to do others.

Right-sided weakness/left-sided stroke Theresa has weakness of the right side from a stroke on the left side of her brain. People with right-sided weakness (hemiplegia or half-weakness) will often have difficulty with speech (aphasia) because the center for speech is on the left side of the brain in right-handed people. Even though Theresa may not be able to speak very well, it does not mean that she cannot write, understand, or communicate in other ways, for example, by acting out her wishes and thoughts. Constantly correcting a person with right-sided weakness and insisting that he or she pronounce words correctly is the wrong approach. If your parent has hemiplegia, the best attitude to take is to just communicate any way you can, using hands, mime, writing, and voice. Use whatever works. Both you and your parent may learn to use a whole new "language."

A common mistake is overestimating a stroke victim's ability to comprehend. Just because your parent smiles and nods does not necessarily mean that he or she understands what you are saying. If you have ever been in a country where a foreign language is spoken, you will remember what it is like. In order to check to see if your parent can understand, simply say, "Please close your eyes." If he or she nods and smiles and makes no attempt to do what you ask, you must assess what exactly your parent does understand.

People with right-sided strokes are usually hesitant and slow to perform what, to them, are now new tasks. It is important to give feedback often and correctly. Break down tasks into component parts. For example, if your father is dressing, lay out his trousers. Ask him to take them and turn them right-side round. Break the task into ten or more different actions. When he does each one correctly, give positive feedback, such as "Well done." If he makes a mistake, give him a chance to correct it first. If he persists, indicate that there has been an error, give a few hints if necessary, and provide feedback again when the mistake has been corrected.

Here are some further tips for managing right-sided weakness. Assess your parent's level of understanding before you start to communicate.

- There is no need to shout.
- Keep it simple—one idea or one step at a time.
- Use short, simple phrases.
- Do not use baby talk.
- Be patient and take your time. It may be slow, but it will be worth it if you find an effective way of communicating.
- Contact a speech therapist to find out alternative ways of communicating.

Left-sided weakness/right-sided stroke Weakness of the left side usually means that the right side of the brain has been damaged. The right side of the brain deals with spatial orientation. People who damage this side often have difficulty judging size, position, and form. They miss the bottom step, jam their wheelchair against the side of the doorway, and miss the table putting back a cup. They may be unable to perform fine movements such as doing up buttons. These problems are easy to mistake, and families often put them down to clumsiness, laziness, or stupidity. Many people with left-sided weakness are not aware of their deficits themselves.

While people with right-sided weakness are slow and deliberate, those with left-sided weakness are usually the opposite. Because they are often unaware of their spatial problems, they tend to overestimate their abilities. People with left-sided weakness need help when learning and performing new tasks. They need to slow down and check each particular step. Break tasks into single steps, and give lots of positive feedback. Watch what can be done safely, and keep the living environment free of clutter.

Neglect Some stroke patients cannot see on one side. This is referred to as "neglect." Those with right-sided weakness tend to have right-sided neglect, while those with left-sided weakness tend to have left-sided neglect. Although many learn to make the adjustment simply by turning their heads, others don't. Some don't recognize one side of their body and may become angry because they think there is somebody else in bed with them. They may eat only from one side of a plate, and people who approach from the "neglected" side may be ignored.

If your parent has this condition, it is important to place anything that you want him or her to pay attention to on the non-neglected side. Situate your parent's bed against the wall, with the neglected side toward the wall and the "good" side facing out into the rest of the room. Arrange items in closets, drawers, and lockers on the non-neglected side. Ribbons or bells can be placed on the neglected half of pieces of clothing to remind your parent of that side's existence. Your parent may also benefit from performing tasks in front of a mirror so that he or she can see both sides of the body again and learn to use the affected side.

Keep reminding your parent about the neglected side, and encourage him or her to be aware of it and to use it as much as possible. Rearrange the furniture and the living environment to facilitate coping.

Memory and emotions People often experience changes in their personality after a stroke. Shy people may become outgoing, and fastidious people may become sloppy and careless. Some of these changes can be helped, but others can't. It is important to set realistic goals in helping your parent with these problems. Many experience difficulty with new learning and short-term memory. They can remember events prior to the stroke but have trouble learning new information afterward.

First, measure how much new information your parent can retain. Many stroke patients cannot follow a three- or four-step command. For example, if asked to take their shoes off, put them under the bed, and lie on the bed, they might take off their shoes and put them under the bed, and just sit there because they have forgotten the third step. If this is the case, it is necessary to break down actions into simple steps. It might even be helpful to write down routine tasks in individual steps so that your parent can follow them more easily and does not have to be prompted.

If your parent can follow only a two-step command, remember this when telling stories and communicating. It may be necessary to tell a story slowly with frequent repetitions to enable your parent to understand it one point at a time. Be sure to allow plenty of time for questions before moving on to a new topic.

It is extremely important to set a routine. The routine is reassuring, and if it is followed regularly, stroke patients get used to it and function better because they know what is expected of them. If there is any change in the routine, they may become confused and irritated, and their ability to function may deteriorate.

Memory aids are very useful. Write down special events, doctor's visits, and so on, on a calendar or diary so that your parent can refer to it. Laying out medications in a prominent place on a sideboard or kitchen table with daily reminders of when to take them is another way to help your parent do as much for him- or herself as possible.

People who have suffered from strokes often have emotional lability. This means their emotions are more labile, or variable and unpredictable. They may start crying or laughing for no apparent reason. Although many of those who cry are actually depressed, some cry even though they are not sad. Your parent may be depressed if he says he cries because he is sad and mourning his losses (see page 57 for information on depression). But if he stops crying suddenly when someone talks to him or his moods change rapidly, he is probably not depressed. Those who are depressed are likely to say, "I was crying because I felt sad," while those who have emotional lability without depression will say, "I just started crying for no reason."

If your parent behaves inappropriately by swearing or having angry outbursts—"You stupid *&$#@, get my socks"—give immediate feedback by saying, "I don't like it when you say things like that. It makes me sad." It is important to say this immediately in a gentle, caring fashion. Saying it later is not as effective. It is also important to be consistent and supportive, not negative and nagging. Provide an alternative at the same time: "Just ask me nicely and say, 'Please get my socks.'"

Here are some other tips for dealing with memory and emotional problems:

- Set a routine and stick to it as much as possible.
- Try to let your parent do as much for him- or herself as possible.
- Keep messages short to make it easier for your parent to remember them.
- Use memory aids such as calendars, diaries, written notes, and step-by-step instructions.
- Give feedback immediately in a positive fashion and offer alternatives.
- Give lots of love and reassurance: "I will always love you and be here for you."
- Finally, remember that nobody is perfect and we all lose our tempers and feel down once in a while. Do your best, and be as honest and open with yourself and your parent as you can be. Keep communicating how you feel, and keep asking how he or she feels.

Some people who have had a stroke experience problems with bladder and/or bowel control, or have difficulty walking and are prone to falling. See the sections on incontinence (page 23) and falls (page 20) for information on these problems.

For further information, contact the American Heart Association, 5575 Thompson Road, Syracuse, NY 13214. Toll-free: 1-800-AHA-USA1; phone: (315) 446-8334.

Mental Health

Loneliness

Jim is a 70-year-old widower who lives in a seniors apartment building. Although he seems happy enough, when his daughter comes to visit, she always finds him alone staring out the window or watching television. When I saw him he wasn't depressed, but he was lonely. Jim had lost all of his friends when he moved out of his house and into the apartment. He had no social contacts and never went out alone. The days were very long and he had trouble sleeping at night.

Watch your parents for signs of loneliness, such as day-dreaming, sleeping too much, and watching too much TV. Too much television watching is a guaranteed way of creating depression and loneliness. And napping during the day leads to trouble sleeping at night.

Children can advise a parent who is lonely to keep busy, become a volunteer, write letters, and visit people. The happiest person I ever met and the busiest person I ever met are one and the same. Suggest that your parent fix something that needs fixing, take up a hobby, and stay involved—often a small project can become a significant one. You can also advise your parent to try to cure the loneliness of someone else; it will cure his own. There are many people who need help. It's just a matter of searching them out.

If your parent is lonely, she may be depressed and unhappy. Here is what she can do to help herself: Fight unhappiness with a direct attack of the will. Ask yourself the question, "How does my unhappiness change my situation?" The answer will be, "It doesn't, it just makes it worse." So make things better by choosing to be happy. Fight depression by talking out your problems. Talk to friends, a counselor, or your pastor or rabbi, and keep talking until you find yourself maintaining an attitude of optimism. Collecting inspirational thoughts, good jokes, meaningful poems, and literary masterpieces can help fight unhappiness. Reading good books or taking out talking books from the library is another good strategy.

Frequently, loneliness occurs at certain times of the day or on specific holidays, birthdays, and anniversaries. Planning ahead to keep active and busy at these times helps to avoid loneliness.

Encourage your parent to join one of the many social groups in her community. See that she visits the senior center regularly and meets new people. She will find many individuals there who are involved in social gatherings of various types. She should commit herself to one or more groups that she finds of interest.

Loneliness is often caused by relying on others to do something for us. However, when we do things for others, we are never lonely. Self-referenced thinking often leads to a barrenness of spirit that breeds discontent and loneliness. I advise older people to "think up, think out, think about all the exciting people and things in your life. Avoid thinking too much about yourself, and the problem of loneliness will disappear."

Some children feel responsible for their parent's loneliness because they are unable to visit as often as they would like. Their parent may complain that they don't visit enough. It's important to supplement visits with phone calls, cards, letters, and other ways of keeping in touch. However, if this is an issue in your family, you should also discuss it with your parent. During this discussion, parents may come to understand that their children have other commitments and appreciate their efforts when they do call or visit. If at all possible, you and your mother or father should agree on a schedule; for example, weekly phone calls or monthly visits. Siblings can work together to spread out their contact with their parent and leave as few gaps as possible.

Emotional Changes

Lynn, a kind, loving daughter, was having a difficult time with her mother, Agnes. Her mother called and asked her to visit all the time, but when Lynn visited, Agnes just complained about her life and became angry. Lynn felt that her mother was unfairly blaming her for her problems. When she went to visit she felt bad, but when she stayed away she felt guilty. She was caught between a rock and a hard place. Lynn's husband, Mario, told her not to visit any more because her mother upset her and did not seem to appreciate her visits.

For most children the worst part of a parent's aging may not be the physical problems but the changes in personality and emotional state. Children can often cope better with physical illnesses than with anxiety, anger, or emotional changes. Physical problems seem more obvious and legitimate. A parent's anxiety, anger, and rejection may be more difficult to understand, accept, and manage.

Lynn became upset when her mother said, "No one ever visits me. I wish I was dead. I feel sick all the time. My whole life is miserable." She felt responsible: "I wish she would realize that it's not my fault. I wish she would change and stop blaming me."

I hear sons and daughters wishing their parents would change all the time. They often feel guilty, blame themselves, and think it's their fault that their parent is unhappy. The problem is that parents usually can't change how they feel. As some parents age, their physical function deteriorates, and then control over their emotional state often diminishes. They become anxious, obsessive, depressed, demanding, or angry.

Agnes was quite forgetful and failing physically. She took her anger and her frustration out on Lynn. This is what I advised Lynn to do:

- Get professional help. Don't try to carry the burden alone. A change in behavior and personality may be a sign of an underlying physical illness, depression, or emotional problem. First, Lynn needs to make sure that the behavior change is not caused by a drug, a medical or psychiatric illness, or another physical problem that can be treated. She did this. She brought her mother to see me for a thorough checkup, and we did find a physical problem.

- Label it. When her mother becomes angry, Lynn could say, "You are very angry, Mom." That way, Lynn acknowledges what she is dealing with. She then must accept that it's not her own or her mother's fault. Agnes is failing physically, mentally, and emotionally. Lynn is experiencing the changes in her mother's emotional control. This is a common accompaniment of a wide variety of physical and mental diseases.

- Lynn must examine how she reacts to her mother. How does the anger make her feel? When Agnes becomes angry or expresses frustration, does Lynn respond by: becoming angry back at her, feeling ashamed, intimidated, or guilty that she should be doing more? Does she feel it's her fault, blame herself, and feel guilty?

  It's important for Lynn to become aware of how this behavior makes her feel physically, psychologically, and emotionally. Does she tighten up, flush, feel nauseated? Does she have a desire to leave or retaliate? I told Lynn to relax, take control of the situation, and not blame her mother.

- Lynn must empathize and not deny her mother's feelings. She could say: "I don't blame you for being angry with this disease. You must be very frustrated because you feel so alone and hopeless."

Lynn needs to realize that her mother is angry with the disease and disability, not necessarily with her. At this stage Lynn should not try to reason with her mother and present solutions by saying "We can fix this if we..." It won't work now, while Agnes is angry and frustrated. Her mother is not ready to listen. Lynn should not deny Agnes the right to feel angry, sad, or frustrated by saying, "I can't understand why you are so angry over this.... It's such a small thing." Nor should Lynn say, "You have no right to treat me like this. I have done nothing to you. Why are you so angry at me?" This is guaranteed to make Agnes even more angry. Lynn's most appropriate response to Agnes, when she is expressing an emotion in such a strong fashion, is to empathize with her. Once Lynn has validated ("I understand why you..." "I don't blame you for...") her mother's feelings, then it is appropriate to try to solve the problem. First she should allow Agnes to vent and then try to calm her down before she starts to suggest solutions.

This was my advice to Lynn:

- Don't argue or get caught in the emotion. Stand back and try to see what's happening. Don't get sucked in. Don't respond with anger because you feel that your mother is attacking you in particular.
- Distract Agnes or change the subject. Introduce a subject that she will find soothing, cheerful, or interesting. Say something like: "You look nice today..." or "Susan called last night," or "The baby is doing fine." Give good news, be cheerful, and stay as positive as possible. Try to calm Agnes down.
- Offer to help. When the emotion has passed, you can then try to help in a practical way—"What can I do to help you?" Now it is time to be logical and try to problem-solve. Ask Agnes what she thinks the problem is, and then try to work on solutions together. Agnes must be part of the solution.

- If this fails, leave and come back. Try: "Excuse me for a few moments, I left something in the car" or "I have to go to the bathroom."
- If Agnes remains angry and cannot be calmed down, then it may be best to leave. "You are very upset today. I will leave and come back when you are feeling better."
- Don't take it personally. Agnes may be nice to strangers and only complain to Lynn, because her daughter may be the only person she feels she can talk to.

As much as Lynn wishes her mother could change and act more like some other older person she knows or some image she has in her mind, Agnes probably never will. Wishing that Agnes would go back to the way she was or that she would become more like Jessica Tandy in *Fried Green Tomatoes* is unrealistic and can be damaging. Agnes would probably like to be pleasant with a great sense of humor, too, instead of being racked by anxiety, anger, and self-pity. The challenge is to stand back and not get dragged into the emotional state.

Don't blame older parents who behave like this. It's not intentional. This type of behavior suggests that the parent is having a problem with depression or anxiety. Of course, if Agnes was abusive all her life and always behaved like this, then it may not be healthy for Lynn to keep exposing herself to this type of abusive behavior. In this case the husband may be right, and I would advise Lynn to leave her alone.

If you are having problems when you visit a parent, analyze it first and develop strategies. Don't ignore it or try to shrug off your parent's emotional problems, and remember, it may not be possible to relieve anxiety, frustration, or anger completely. The best you may be able to do is say, "I understand and I will be here for you." That may be enough.

I took Lynn's husband aside and gave him the same advice I always give to spouses who are caught up in this type of situation. The bond between a parent and child is a powerful one. It is best to keep clear and not get involved. He should try to support Lynn and not criticize her or her mother. They are both trapped in this relationship. If he tries to persuade Lynn to stop visiting her mother, she may continue and stop telling him how she is suffering. If this happens, she will lose her greatest support. If he is worried, he should get professional advice. If Agnes or Lynn doesn't like what the doctor says, she can change doctors. However, if Lynn doesn't like what Mario says, she may be tempted to change husbands. Doctors are likely to be more objective and able to see the problem from both perspectives.

Spouses who play the psychiatrist can be blamed in the end. If Lynn stops visiting her mother, she may feel guilty later and blame Mario. In short, listen, support, and try to stay out of it. Offer advice only when asked for it. If Mario really feels that his wife's health is in danger, he could be right, but he should seek professional advice. He should let the doctor advise his wife about what to do.

Memory Loss

Louise went to her daughter Barbara's new home for Christmas dinner. She asked where the bathroom was. Barbara gave her directions, but Louise had to ask the way each time she had to go and kept getting lost. Finally Barbara said, "Mom, what's the matter with you? I've told you fifty times already." Louise became angry, said she was going to walk home, and stormed out of the house into a blizzard without her coat.

It's not unusual for families to first notice that a parent is failing as a result of an event like this. Louise had probably been losing her memory for years but was able to cover up successfully in her own home. In her daughter's home, she failed to remember a simple set of directions to the bathroom. This inability to learn new information exposed her memory problem. Barbara may have noticed that her mother was having problems, but just put it down to old age. But now Louise's behavior and inappropriate response are a warning sign that must be heeded.

Louise is very sensitive to any criticism about her failing memory. She overreacted to the comment about her memory problems and may be worried that she has Alzheimer's disease. There is a problem that needs attention.

The first signs of aging may come on gradually but become unmasked in a sudden, catastrophic way. For most of us, aging causes a gradual decline in energy, vision, or hearing. We stop taking chances, lack spontaneity, and change attitudes.

Many conditions can cause memory loss, and some of them can be cured. About 10 to 20 percent of older people who develop memory loss have a reversible condition. It is important to remember that not all cases of memory loss are caused by Alzheimer's disease. Memory loss can be caused by an underactive thyroid or vitamin deficiency. It can also be caused by over-the-counter or prescribed drugs. Once use of the drugs is discontinued, the person can remember again. Many of the drugs older people take can have side effects that may be worse than the disease. There is an epidemic of overprescribing to the elderly; many have their quality of life ruined by drugs that they don't even need.

As we age, we slow down mentally and physically. Just compare an old person and a teenager learning to play a video game that requires quick reactions and fine eye–hand coordination; the differences are obvious. But observe them play Scrabble or a game that requires general knowledge and the older person will win almost every time.

Although aging slows us down mentally, it is not normally associated with serious memory loss. Old people become forgetful and misplace things, and have problems finding the right word sometimes, but they can remember their children's names and where they live. They may not care what day of the week it is, but they can function.

Memory loss that impairs a person's ability to function is not a normal part of aging. Serious memory loss is a disease, not a normal or inevitable part of aging.

Depression and Anxiety

Retirement and loss of a spouse and friends can diminish social contacts and supports, leading to isolation and depression. Men aged 65 to 74 have the highest risk of suicide in the general population. Although depression is common and treatable, it often goes undetected by family members and health-care providers. However, once they are aware of the warning signs of depression, they can play a critical role in identifying elders at risk and supplying information and timely referral to appropriate services.

Depression can sometimes mimic Alzheimer's and is so frequently misdiagnosed as dementia that the condition has been called "pseudodementia," or false dementia. There are certain clues that suggest depression is causing an older person's deterioration in function. Claire is a typical example.

Claire, a 79-year-old widow, lives alone in her own house. When her son Greg came to visit, he became concerned because the house was untidy and the fridge was empty. His mother had stopped going out to visit friends and had become withdrawn and socially isolated. She was more forgetful and had given up doing the crossword, which she had done daily for the past forty years.

Claire talked a lot about the miscarriage she had had after Greg was born. Her husband had died two years previously and she still cried when she talked about him. She said he often appeared when she was falling asleep or waking up in the morning. Her doctor had prescribed new pills for her high blood pressure about three months earlier, but she wanted to stop taking them because she said she didn't care if she lived or died.

Although Claire had always enjoyed visits from her children and grandchildren in the past, now she said the grandchildren were too noisy and she didn't want to see them. She complained that she wasn't sleeping and had lost her appetite. She had also lost weight. Her diet consisted of tea and toast. She called Greg one day and complained that there was a blockage in her bowels.

Greg seems to remember that his mother went through something like this when he was younger.

Greg was concerned. He thought his mother had Alzheimer's disease. Some of Claire's symptoms, like forgetfulness, are also Alzheimer's symptoms. Is she growing old and becoming more rigid and difficult, or is she depressed?

Almost 40 percent of men and more than 25 percent of women can expect to develop a psychiatric disorder over the course of their lifetime. One in ten people (7 percent of men and 13 percent of women) suffer from depression, and 11 percent suffer from an anxiety disorder *at any one time.*

Depression and anxiety are symptoms of an underlying problem. Broadly speaking, there are two types of depression: reactive (a reaction to a life event) or endogenous (occurs for no apparent reason and probably results from spontaneous chemical changes in the brain). Reactive depression may be caused by alcohol or drug abuse; a medical illness; or reaction to loss, death, or separation. Depression and anxiety are more common in some families, and those who have a family history of depression are more likely to be affected. Over-the-counter and prescribed drugs can also cause depression or anxiety. Caffeine, stimulants, and sleep loss can worsen anxiety.

Symptoms of depression are the most common psychiatric problems in older people. Up to 10 percent of men and 15 percent of women aged 65 and over suffer from depression. Old age is a time of loss. The elderly lose freedom, vitality, and independence. They are more likely to develop diseases that are associated with pain, disability, and suffering. As losses accumulate, even a fairly trivial one can trigger depression, like the straw that breaks the camel's back.

Parkinson's, Alzheimer's, and strokes are commonly associated with depression. People with these diseases often respond to their loss of function by becoming depressed. In these cases, depression coexists with the disease and adds to the disability. Although there may be no effective treatment or cure for some of the underlying illnesses, treatment of the depression results in a major improvement in the person's quality of life and function.

Drugs can also trigger depression. The use of prescription and non-prescription drugs is high among the elderly. Seniors, who make up about 10 percent of the population, use 30 percent of all prescription drugs dispensed. Older adults experience more drug side effects and toxicity because they cannot clear drugs from the body as quickly as younger people can. A good rule of thumb is that every drug can potentially trigger depression and should be suspected as a potential cause.

A number of clues suggest that Claire has depression.

"Her doctor had prescribed new pills for her high blood pressure about three months earlier." It was around this time that Greg first noticed a change in his mother. When an older person becomes depressed, first suspect a reaction to a drug. If the depression started around the time the new drug started, stop it, if possible, and substitute something else. Greg should report this to the family doctor so his mother's high blood pressure pills can be stopped or changed. The substitution of another drug may make all the difference.

Family doctors frequently miss depression because it can present itself in so many different ways, from dramatic, impulsive, or manipulative behavior to withdrawal, apathy, and self-neglect. Doctors trained in Western medicine are taught to assign a physical cause for all their patients' ills. They often waste valuable time and resources doing the "million-dollar workup" on depressed people, trying to find a physical cause for their problems. The psychological symptoms and clues are missed because they are falsely attributed to physical causes. In many cases, doctors spend too little time with their patients to explore their problems properly. Even patients with physical problems deteriorate or fail to respond to treatment if they are depressed. Instead of spending time trying to get to the root of the problem, physicians order more tests and drugs for each new symptom, while the underlying cause, depression, is overlooked, even masked.

People with medical problems who become depressed are more likely to complain of worsening of their physical problems than of memory or mood changes. These complaints are often attributed to the medical condition. For example, doctors often mistake worsening arthritis, angina, or shortness of breath to progression of the disease, when in fact the person has become depressed. The doctor increases the doses of the medications for these problems, but the patient has little relief. If the underlying problem, depression, is missed, the problems will persist.

In an older person, when there is deterioration in function without any obvious physical cause, consider depression. The depressed elderly are more likely to lose weight and often don't report mood changes or feelings of worthlessness or guilt. Many will not admit they are depressed because they are afraid they will be locked away or ignored. They think depressed people are "crazy" and are sent to the "loony bin." Depression is not seen as a legitimate problem; it is considered a weakness.

Depression is often mistaken for Alzheimer's disease. The symptoms of this type of depression are usually changes in attention, concentration, and memory. In younger people, these changes are more easily recognized as signs of depression. In the elderly, they are often inappropriately blamed on "senility." In depression, the loss in cognitive function is often patchy and inconsistent, and progresses over a relatively short period of months. In Alzheimer's disease, the memory loss comes on slowly over years and does not vary much. The person suffers from memory loss, then gets depressed. In depression, the mood change comes before the memory loss; the person gets depressed, then starts to lose his or her memory.

Depressed people are often aware of their memory loss. They are likely to point out their memory lapses and to exaggerate their disability. People with Alzheimer's often lack insight into their memory problems and are more inclined to deny memory loss. Those with Alzheimer's try, when requested to perform tasks or answer questions. They frequently have near misses. For example, when you ask them what year it is, they will try, "Is it 1954?" The depressed person is likely to say, "Leave me alone. I'm useless. I can't do anything. Don't waste your time." They know the answer but can't be bothered answering.

An antidepressant drug, even in low doses, can bring about dramatic improvement. When the depression is treated, the person with depression can return to normal or near normal. Depressed Alzheimer's patients can also have a remarkable improvement in their quality of life if they are treated.

The biggest problem in making a diagnosis of depression is often the physician's or family's bias in thinking: "It's just his age, what do you expect?" or "Anybody would be depressed in her situation." In these cases, the depression is overlooked because the symptoms and/or signs are attributed to the underlying chronic disease or advancing age. But many older people deal very well with illness and disability. Depression is not a normal or inevitable consequence of disease or aging, and it should be treated.

"Claire had stopped going out to visit friends ... and had given up doing the crossword." Persistent anhedonia (loss of interest or enjoyment in all activities that previously gave pleasure) is very suggestive of depression. Claire has

stopped visiting her friends and no longer enjoys hobbies that previously gave her pleasure. She doesn't want the children or grandchildren to visit. Her son's visit didn't cheer her up. Lonely people usually cheer up when people visit. Depressed people don't. They tend to stay depressed.

"She complained that she wasn't sleeping." Depressed people report that the quality of their sleep is disrupted and unsatisfactory. They have difficulty falling off to sleep and wake often during the night or early in the morning. They often feel exhausted in the morning and do not get any rest or renewal from sleep. They improve as the day progresses. In depression, the mood is often worse in the morning; people with physical illness usually feel better after a night's rest and become tired later in the day.

If Claire experienced a sudden change in her sleep pattern, it would strongly suggest depression. If she has been a poor sleeper all her life, then depression is probably not the cause. Of course, it would also be important to find out if she is waking up because of pain or because she has to go to the bathroom.

"Greg seems to remember that his mother went through something like this when he was younger." Has Claire had previous episodes of depression? Has she been treated by a psychiatrist or admitted to an institution in the past? Did she ever miss work for prolonged periods with a vague or undiagnosed illness?

If she had a previous episode of depression, Greg should help the doctor obtain old medical charts to establish the diagnosis, medications used, and what worked. A previous episode after a traumatic event, childbirth, or just out of the blue makes it more likely that Claire is suffering from depression now.

"The house was untidy and the fridge was empty. She had stopped going out to visit friends and had become with-

drawn." Depression is often associated with changes in activity levels. Some depressed people have decreased activity—withdrawal, apathy, a change in normal daily routines and function. Others have increased activity, with pacing, hand wringing, panic, and anxiety. Claire has slowed down. She is not taking care of her house and has stopped attending social outings.

Depressed seniors are often given sedatives for anxiety or sleep problems. Since it takes them longer to clear these from their system, they may be groggy during the day and unable to care for themselves. If depression causes the sleep problems in the first place, sedatives will mask the condition. This can contribute further to apathy and withdrawal. They should be treated for the depression.

"She called Greg one day and complained that there was a blockage in her bowels." The belief that there is a blockage in her bowels is a delusion. Delusions are relatively common in depressed older people and are frequently missed ,by family and medical practitioners. Older patients often feel ashamed or afraid of their delusions, and do not talk about them easily or spontaneously.

There are several different types of delusions. With delusions of poverty, people believe that they have no money, or that their property or savings are gone. In hospital, they often believe they are going to be thrown out because they cannot pay their bills. With delusions of persecution, they believe they are being tortured or poisoned by family members, health professionals, or neighbors. The injections and blood work they receive in modern hospitals often reinforce these beliefs. Older men and women may even have delusions of nihilism where they believe that parts of their body are missing, that they are dead, or that they don't exist any more. Some believe they are being punished for wrongs that they have committed in the past. The feature of these delusions that points to depression is that they believe they deserve whatever they think is happening to them.

Often depressed seniors slow down and become constipated and obsessed with their bowels. They think food is rotting inside or that they have cancer. Claire believes she has a bowel blockage. She is describing a physical complaint that may have no apparent physical basis. Depression may be associated with loss of appetite and weight loss, even suggesting malignancy in the bowel. Despite the "million-dollar workup," the person may remain convinced that doctors are hiding something or have missed something. It is important to consider depression in these cases.

"Her husband died two years previously. She said he often appeared when she was falling asleep or waking up in the morning." These appearances are called "hypnagogic hallucinations." They are very common, and many who have lost a loved one report seeing the dead person at the foot of the bed when they are falling asleep or waking up. Many older people talk to their dead children and spouses, the television, or photos. This is often reassuring, is not harmful, and doesn't require treatment. Children can reassure a parent that this is perfectly normal. She should not be discouraged from talking to the visions unless she is becoming disturbed or frightened, or the visions are telling her to harm herself or others.

"She talks a lot about the miscarriage she had after Greg was born." Depressed elders' thoughts are filled with feelings of uselessness and guilt. They dredge up all of their sad experiences and go over them again and again. Unpleasant events that may have happened many years ago resurface, and they will often blame themselves for them. All losses are connected, and a recent loss, such as a change in eyesight or hearing, or not being issued a driving license, can trigger depression. Previous losses surface and seem to overwhelm the person.

"She still cries when she talks about her husband. She doesn't care if she lives or dies." A heart patient with

angina often remarks that the pain from a heart attack had a different intensity and quality from normal angina pain. The pain was much worse, lasted longer, and did not go away during a period of rest. In a similar fashion, a person with depression may describe sadness as being like a cloud or heaviness that can't be lifted. It is not the usual sadness or grief that has accompanied a death or other tragedy. It often has a distinct quality that is overpowering.

The depression is often associated with a physical feeling of weight pressing down on them or a feeling of unease, anxiety, or impending doom. In older people, this feeling is often located in the abdomen, which leads to the conviction that there is something wrong inside. This may develop to the point where they believe there is a blockage, or food rotting inside, or a cancerous growth.

Claire is still mourning her husband. It is now two years since his death. Although the mourning process is prolonged in her case, some people mourn for a lifetime. Most will have worked through their grief in a few years. Grief does not require treatment unless it is interfering with a person's health or function.

In any depressed elder it is important to establish what risk, if any, there is of suicide. The vast majority of those who commit suicide are depressed. The risk of suicide rises sharply in depressed widowed males. If your parent has thought about suicide, or if he has suicidal urges, it is important to discuss this with him. Suicidal urges usually frighten the people who experience them. If you have ever been on a tall building, looked down, and been uncomfortable because you have had a desire to jump, you will understand what a suicidal urge is like. These urges, which can come weekly, daily, or even more often, are uncomfortable and threatening.

If your parent has suicidal urges and feels that he cannot cope with them, or if he seems to be making a plan, then urgent assessment and supervision are warranted. Comments like "You won't have to worry about me any longer" should be taken seriously and reported to his family doctor. Likewise, if he is storing pills, he requires urgent treatment. Depressed seniors usually succeed when they try to kill themselves.

When asking about suicide, it is best to be honest and straightforward. Just ask, "Have you ever considered killing yourself?" or "Have you ever wished you were dead?" If your parent says, "Yes, but I would never do it because it would shame the family" or "God would punish me," the risk is small.

"Her diet consisted of tea and toast." The elderly often experience loss of appetite when they become depressed. Many older people cannot afford to lose weight, and this symptom must be attended to quickly. Antidepressants help the appetite; in fact, this is one of their most important effects.

FEATURES OF DEPRESSION

- Depressed or sad mood, or loss of interest and pleasure in most usual activities.
- Four of the following for more than two weeks:
  - poor appetite or significant weight loss, or increased appetite or significant weight gain;
  - insomnia or hypersomnia (sleeping all the time);
  - loss of energy;
  - physical agitation or slowing down;
  - anhedonia (loss of interest or pleasure in usual activities) and decreased sex drive;
  - feelings of self-reproach or inappropriate guilt;
  - diminished ability to think or concentrate;
  - suicidal ideas.
- Syndrome not part of schizophrenia or paranoid disorder.
- None of these dominate the picture for more than three months after the onset of the depression: preoccupation with delusions or hallucinations; obvious thought disorders; or bizarre or grossly disorganized behavior.

Adapted from American Psychiatric Association, *DSMIII* (Washington, 1982).

Treating depression Depressed older adults often experience a deterioration in their everyday functioning. Claire, for example, cannot keep her house clean, shop, cook, or maintain herself. She has stopped eating properly and is losing weight. She may stop taking medications for other medical conditions and deteriorate physically. If she stops eating she will become malnourished, and if she stops taking her medications she will experience further functional and physical decline, unless something is done soon.

At this stage, it is important to arrange for Meals on Wheels, visiting homemakers, nurses, or other help in the house. Claire needs to be supervised in the short term to make sure she is eating properly and taking her medications. She will not be able to live at home much longer if she continues to be unable to cope. She should receive treatment.

The first step in treating depression is to withdraw any medications that may be causing a person's depression. This alone may solve the problem. Next, a thorough physical examination and some blood-screening tests will be given to rule out any physical cause. The doctor will then try to find out if there is some other reason why the person has become depressed. Did the cat die? Did her friend stop visiting, or did she misplace her dentures? Did something that seems fairly trivial to others, but may be very important to her, happen? The solution may be as simple as replacing her dentures, getting a new prescription for her glasses so she can read again, or getting another cat.

If the person remains depressed after her medications have been withdrawn, or substituted, she may require treatment with an antidepressant. Older adults have an increased risk of side effects from all drugs, so her doctor must ensure that an antidepressant drug won't make her worse. Antidepressants often take two to three weeks before any effects are seen. A group of drugs called tricyclic antidepressants were the drug of choice for the treatment of depression in seniors. Recently, however, they have been replaced by the SSRI group (serotonin-specific reuptake inhibitors).

Tricyclic antidepressants This group of drugs is still widely used in the treatment of major depression in later life. Nortryptiline, which is sedating, is used for elderly depressed people with sleep disturbance. The starting dose is usually 10 milligrams at night, with the dose increasing by 10 milligrams every few weeks until a response occurs or side effects limit further increases. Doses of 50 to 75 milligrams are usually sufficient, but many older patients respond to even lower doses. Desipramine is less sedating and can be given during the day. Close monitoring is essential. Tricyclics may cause confusion, constipation, urinary retention, and dry mouth. They can also cause the blood pressure to fall on standing and increase the risk of falls.

Serotonin antagonists (SSRIs) This relatively new group of antidepressants includes fluoxetine hydrochloride (Prozac), sertraline (Zoloft), fluvoxamine maleate (Luvox), and paroxetine hydrochloride (Paxil). Generally, these drugs are well tolerated in younger people and in the elderly. They certainly have a place in the treatment of depression.

Tetracyclic antidepressants Trazodone and maprotiline, two tetracyclic antidepressants, are useful for patients who cannot tolerate tricyclics. Trazodone is started at 50 milligrams at night and increased by 50-milligram increments, until 200 to 300 milligrams is given or until patients develop side effects. Patients frequently develop drowsiness or dizziness. These agents are not well tolerated in the elderly.

Lithium Lithium carbonate may be prescribed to older people with manic depression or to those who have failed to respond to tricyclics or tetracyclics.

Monoamine oxidase inhibitors (MAOI) A new class of MAOIs has recently been developed. These are MAOIa and MAOIb. The older MAOIs required special diets that did not contain tyramine (red wine or cheese). The new MAOIs do not require a special diet and are fairly well tolerated in the elderly. Examples are brofaromine, moclobemide, and L-deprenyl. Moclobemide (Manerix) may be particularly useful for older people because it avoids a lot of the unpleasant side effects associated with tricyclics.

Psychostimulants A dose of 5 to 10 milligrams of methylphenindate (Ritalin) in the morning has been used to augment the tricyclics, particularly in depressed seniors who are withdrawn and apathetic. The dose may be increased to up to 10 milligrams three times per day.

Electroconvulsive therapy (ECT) This may be very useful in older people, particularly those with psychotic depression and those who are more likely to have troublesome limiting side effects with drug treatment. In refractory depression, where there is an acute suicidal risk, or where there is an acute physical deterioration from neglect or anorexia, ECT may be the treatment of choice. Unfortunately, the film *One Flew Over the Cuckoo's Nest* tarnished the reputation of ECT. But, in truth, for some people it can have an instant, life-saving effect.

Neuroleptics These are used in addition to tricyclics or other medications where there are delusions or hallucinations. There are many different agents on the market, but it is advisable to start with Mellaril 10 milligrams, Pimozide 1 milligram, Haloperidol 0.25 milligram, or Loxepine 5 milligrams at night or twice daily. These doses can be increased gradually, depending on side effects or the individual's response.

Even if your parent has an underlying illness like Alzheimer's disease, treatment of depression may lift her mood; improve her sleep, appetite, and energy; and cause a dramatic improvement in her quality of life.

2
Coming to Terms
with Aging

I saw my mother as a bitter old woman who was determined to make me suffer and feel guilty. She called me up constantly just to complain. She never seemed to take pleasure in anything.

One day I went to visit her and found her stooped over, picking irises from her garden. Her fingers were deformed and stiff, her back crooked and rigid. She straightened, and caressed the flowers gently as she arranged them. Something about that gesture triggered a memory of her long ago arranging irises on the kitchen table.

Although the years had bent and misshaped her, I saw my mother again, the woman who had nursed and loved me with such tenderness and care. In recent years she hadn't measured up to my image of an ideal elder. She had disappointed me and I had rejected her. Each time she had phoned, my impatience, frustration, and resentment must have been obvious to her. This must have hurt her a great deal; such ingratitude for her endless love and attention.

Slowly she carried the flowers into the house. I was transfixed. Tears filled my eyes and I saw through the tears that she was growing old and feeble. I realized I had been projecting my own fear of aging onto her.

I went into the house and we talked. I apologized and let go of the resentment, anger, and frustration. I finally accepted her growing old and my growing older. I accepted the passage of time.

> *Honor your father and your mother, as Yahweh your God has commanded you so that you may have long life and may prosper in the land that Yahweh your God gives you.*
>
> DEUTERONOMY

Children who care for aging parents find they must take on new roles and new responsibilities. There is an expectation that children will help their aging parents and pay back the debt they owe for the care they received in childhood. This interdependency bonds the different generations together and benefits society. However, children and families respond in very different ways to this expectation.

More and more "empty nests" are being filled by aging parents. They are also being filled by children who move home because of divorce, economic necessity, or illness. The traditional family, with mother at home and father working, is in danger of extinction. Divorce and remarriage connect and cobble families into diverse configurations. We live in, children are reared in, and parents age in a wide variety of different family situations. As the population ages, four or even five generations are alive at the same time, expanding ties between the generations even more.

Healthy, functional families adapt to the changing needs of their members. In spite of tensions and disagreements, these families can work out their problems. The family provides a safety net, a place where its members will always be accepted, secure, and loved. The bonds are resilient enough to resist life's disappointments and tragedies.

Unhealthy or dysfunctional families can't manage stress or adapt to change. Their insecure and threatened members blame one another for any problems that arise and are unable to support one another. Stuck with inflexible rules and locked into fixed behavior patterns, they can't solve their problems or work out solutions.

The Parent–Child Relationship

John took early retirement. His wife, Rita, continued working as a secretary because they needed the money. They had three adult children who lived in different cities. When John developed Alzheimer's, Rita covered for him. They stopped visiting the children and discouraged the children from visiting them. Whenever the kids wanted to visit, Rita always had an excuse why they shouldn't.

The children worried about their father but were busy with their own lives, and often felt relieved when their mother told them not to visit. John stopped answering the phone and Rita always talked for him. As he became more and more confused, he began wandering off and was frequently brought home by the police. He got up at night and wanted to go to the office. Finally, Rita had to lock him in his room at night. She was too proud to ask for help. She tried to manage on her own because she didn't want to burden the children. She told them they were busy with their own lives and reassured them every time they tried to help.

One day John attacked Rita when she tried to stop him from leaving the house. She had a heart attack. He was admitted to the local hospital's psychiatric unit and she was taken to the Intensive Care Unit. She died before the children arrived. Their father was admitted to a nursing home. The children were left to sort out the emotional, financial, and psychological mess left behind. There was no advance directive (living will), will, or power of attorney, and the house carried a mortgage. The parents' affairs were put into the hands of the Public Trustee and the children were left wondering why their parents never contacted or confided in them. They were left with a legacy of unanswered questions and guilt.

Although well-meaning, Rita had unknowingly damaged her children. The children had been denied the opportunity to help their father in his illness. They would now face their own old age dreading what it might hold. By not showing them how to deal with illness and death, she had deprived them of an important and vital experience. The tragedy is that the situation was avoidable.

Parents talk to children about almost everything else, but for many families, the subjects of aging and death are still taboo. Society's reluctance to deal with these issues in an open, frank, and honest way has left us all lacking a mythology, tradition, or template for such discussions. We have stories, books, and films about birth, childhood, marriage, and death. But parents do not routinely prepare their sons and daughters for their own aging and death. Children and parents need to acknowledge and prepare together for these two perfectly natural events.

Unfortunately, many children don't deal well with their parents. The child and parent come from different generations at different phases in the life cycle and find it hard to fathom each other. Trying to communicate, to bridge this generation gap, is like two people with Walkmans, one listening to a waltz, the other to rock-'n'-roll, trying to dance together at the same time. As hard as they try, it's difficult to communicate feelings and say those things they want to say.

Children would like to have a better relationship with their parents but often can't seem to manage it. Although we think of ourselves as rational beings, most of the time we react emotionally and afterwards try to understand and rationalize why we felt or acted the way we did. Parents trigger deep primal feelings over which the children may have little control. Most of the time the children are not even consciously aware of why they felt or reacted as they did. The source of these emotions is hidden deep within the self. Like that little voice inside saying "Call home, call home," children don't know where it comes from. It's like an echo bouncing around in the underground caverns and tectonic plates of the mind. It makes the children feel uneasy and makes it difficult for them to understand why they can't communicate with their parents as well as they would wish. The emotions create a fog, a background noise.

Parents also want to have a better relationship with their children. But boundaries become blurred as the parent and child move through the passages in the life cycle. The parents' passage into old age requires that the relationship evolve and change. It's difficult, however, for both parties to draw the line between ignoring and smothering each other.

For children, it's like an itch they can't scratch. Children feel guilty when they don't call enough, give enough, or visit enough. Many communicate only on holidays and special occasions. No matter how hard children try with gifts, visits, phone calls, or cards, it seems to work only for a short while. Children and parents never seem to be able to say those things they want to say, to have that conversation that they have rehearsed in their minds so many times. It's always the same old feeling of dissatisfaction.

So how can we feel good about our parents? When is enough enough? Does it have to be like this? Is there a solution? The answer is a resounding "Yes." But first we need to understand why we feel this way. We can't delegate the management of this relationship. We must work it out for ourselves. When we have problems with our cars, houses, gardens, pets, or income tax, we can hand them over to an "expert." The yellow pages are full of expert services catering to our every need. When our tennis, windsurfing, or golf game needs help, there are new argon, boron, titanium, or graphite reinforced rackets or the latest special air-adjusted shoes to limit torsional rigidity and add extra bounce. There is a whole range of sports, music, and leisure gizmos to boost our performance, enjoyment, and sensation. There are limitless enhanced, improved, and faster ways to play, travel, feel, or enjoy life. But there are no short cuts when it comes to dealing with parents.

Eric Konigsberg reported how some rich and famous people hire others to perform their mundane tasks for them. When George Bush was campaigning to become President of the United States, he was talking to someone at a supermarket checkout counter when he was startled by the noise of the scanner. He hadn't been in a supermarket for years and had never seen or heard a scanner before. Actress Elizabeth Taylor has apparently never set foot inside a bank. When former U.S. Secretary of State Henry Kissinger walked his dog, one of his bodyguards followed with the pooper-scooper. The rich can hire people to do almost anything. But do you think they could hire someone to visit Mother when she is sick or dying? Can you imagine the phone call: "Mom, I'm really busy right now, so I'm sending over my very own, extra-personal private assistant and look-alike instead." Unlikely, you say?

Some Japanese entrepreneurs are actually working on a solution for busy "successful" people who don't have time for their parents. The Japanese can call an employment agency who, for a price, will send out an actor to impersonate you during a visit to your parents. Presumably, this leaves more time to work and get ahead.

But is there a limit to what can be delegated, to what the hired help can do? Others can't deal with our intimate relationships for us. They can advise and help, but we need to work through these personal issues ourselves.

One of the most powerful forces dictating our emotional responses is attachment behavior. It is the first behavior shown by many different species and seems to be embroidered into our genes. It drives behavior from the cradle to the grave. This is the little voice telling you to phone home.

Attachment behavior is striking in some species. Shortly after hatching, if ducklings and goslings see a large moving object, that image is fixed in their brains and, from then on, they are irreversibly attached to it. This phenomenon is called "imprinting." The young birds follow the object around, try to stay near it, and show distress if they are separated from it. Apes and monkeys cling to their mothers in infancy. Throughout their childhood, they are either in direct contact with them or are very close by. As they grow older, they spend less and less time in direct contact.

Our first and greatest attachment is to our parents. Our relationship with them is the most important and intense in our lives. The loss of parents threatens and frightens us more than any other.

In adolescence, attachment shifts from parents to peers. Each of us believes in some part of our being that we are the sons and daughters of kings and queens and we have somehow landed mistakenly in our dumb families. We dream of being first in the world at sports, painting masterpieces, writing bestsellers, starring in movies. We reject our family, unable to accept their limitations and boring lives. They don't understand or appreciate us. Others shame us: "Who do you think you are? You're too big for your boots." We break free. Breaking free may wound us, though, and some never recover from the wounds or forgive their parents.

Relationships represent a series of attachments and disengagements from friends, lovers, causes, organizations, groups, and ideas. There is an enormous emotional expenditure around this behavior. Behavior patterns learned in childhood determine our responses to change or stress.

As surely as a potter creates a piece of pottery, parents form children and continue to influence them throughout life. Each person's first experience of self is based on his or her child–parent relationship. The deeper and more complete the parental bond, the fuller the child's emotional development. Parents provide a mirror for children to see themselves and a telescopic lens to look ahead into the future.

As we age, we begin to understand that we share our parents' fate. If our parents handle their aging and death successfully, we feel prepared for our own. If they handle it badly, we face our own aging with fear and trepidation.

The members of many families do not live in close proximity. Children may be scattered across countries and continents. Caring for parents from such distances is stressful and demanding. Even those who live near their parents may feel angry and guilty because they resent their parents' demands and intrusions. Other children don't want to even think, let alone talk, about setting limits for their parents. Guilt and a sense of duty force them to take on new responsibilities and obligations to try to pay off the debt they feel is owed.

Responding out of guilt causes its own set of problems. Nobody benefits from care grudgingly given. Parents who feel rejected may become even more demanding and dependent. It can become a vicious circle.

The goal is to find a balance that allows older relatives to live independently at a cost to children that they are prepared to pay. Children often care for their parents through long periods of dependency. Some give up their lives and make incredible sacrifices, yet they still feel that they didn't do enough. Their parents may seem ungrateful, causing their children to feel resentful and angry. This can destroy children, families, and even the children's marriages. After a parent's death, these children may not experience any relief, but instead transfer and direct their frustration and anger at others. They see themselves as victims and learn nothing from the experience. For others in this situation, their relationship with their parents grows and develops and they gain greater insight and control over their own lives. They cherish **and** support their parents and pursue their own happiness without being smothered or overwhelmed by their mothers and fathers. Their parents' death is a positive experience and brings the family closer together.

Understanding Our Parents

If children want to help their parents, first they must understand what happens to people in old age, what they are going through, and what they are thinking. This stage of life brings its own particular problems and challenges. To share the last dance with your mother and father, you need to know what is going on in their heads.

The life cycle is a series of stages through which humans pass. Each stage has an event or crisis that must be resolved before proceeding to the next. We live like travelers facing different challenges and obstacles at each turn. To develop normally and reach the end of our journey, we must overcome the obstacles at each stage. Those who succeed find meaning and satisfaction. Those who fail drag along the unresolved issues from the previous stage and are unable to deal with the obstacles in the next stage. Their journey is burdensome and difficult. These people may gather riches, friends, position, and power, but they are needy and will never feel complete or at peace.

The final stage in human development, known as old age, refers to the period of life after age 75. Erikson described it as a time of conflict between integrity and despair. Integrity is the sense of satisfaction one feels from a life well lived. Despair results from the feeling that life has had little purpose or meaning. Older adults have time to reflect on and contemplate the fruits of their energy and labor, time to watch their life's work being used by the next generation.

Successful older adults accept their place in the life cycle, take responsibility for their life, and believe it has been meaningful. For many, life takes on a magical fragility. They face death willingly, knowing that this is a natural process, which makes perfect sense. They are happy to let the next generation take over. For them old age is a time of fulfillment and joy.

Those who have not managed well during the earlier

stages of life remain stuck in the past. They have not come to terms with life, blame others for misfortune, and spend their time thinking "if only, if only." They are neither ready nor prepared for old age or its consequences. For them it's a frightening time because of their inability to deal with their impending frailty and death.

Some people who do not accept the changes old age brings become depressed, anxious, and desperate. They feel alone, hopeless, and inconsolable. They want to go back to the past and try to change what can't be changed. They judge themselves and find themselves wanting. Old age can be a harsh sentence.

Over all, the elderly are less uniform in behavior than individuals at any other stage of the life cycle. They are more individual and less predictable. They have shifted attachments many times during their lives: from mother and father, to brothers, sisters, peers, career, spouse, family, organizations, ideas, and possessions. Older adults are attached to a wider variety of objects and ideas than other age groups: the past, memories, possessions, home, family, self, causes, and organizations. They spend more time talking about the past than the future. Many remain attached to an image of themselves as young people and can't accept that they have lost vigor, looks, and vitality.

Since old age is a time of multiple losses, the struggle at this stage is to maintain self-esteem and meaning in spite of these losses. Older adults need good health, communal supports, economic security, and self-esteem to cope and continue to function. If any of these are lacking, then the older adult is at increased risk of depression, anxiety, and even suicide. Older adults need to deal with the grief over the loss of friends and loved ones and learn to come to terms with their own loss of control and impending death. They need to resolve the conflict over what they were and what they are. They must deal with their legacy and decide what they wish to leave behind to succeeding generations.

Adult children need to accept their parents for what they

are and how they have lived. Children need to feel that their parents' lives have been worthwhile; if they don't, parents can become overwhelmed with a sense of despair and contempt for themselves and their life's work.

Judging Our Parents

The Brothers Grimm told the story of an old man whose eyes had grown dim and his ears deaf. At the table he could hardly hold his spoon, so he spilled food and drooled. His son and daughter-in-law made him sit in a corner behind the stove. They gave him barely enough food to survive. He used to sit crying at his little table. One day he dropped his bowl and it broke. The young woman scolded him and gave him a cheap wooden replacement. As he ate, his grandson began fitting sticks together on the floor.

"What are you doing with those sticks?" his father asked.

"I'm making a wooden trough for you and Mother to eat from when you grow old," the child replied.

The father and mother began to weep. They immediately brought the old man back to the table and never complained again when he spilled his food.

The relationships with self and others cause misery or happiness. They define us as humans. The relationship with parents is the oldest and most important. Parents exist deep in the most intimate part of self. Childhood experiences create the foundation of the child. In the family the child learns to think, communicate, act, and feel. Over a lifetime we live in several different families acquired through relationships. Understanding the relationships in the first family is necessary to understand the self. If we don't understand what happened in the past, we can fail to resolve issues in the family; this can cause suffering. Most of us first experience aging and death through our parents. These experiences fundamentally and profoundly affect us. This relationship must be approached thoughtfully, with caution, respect, delicacy, and discipline.

We all judge our parents. Many children are angry with their mothers and fathers. Others idolize them. Some children blame parents for their own failures in work, relationships, or life in general. How realistic is this? How much of this is imagined or just an excuse to rationalize failures? The controversy around memories of childhood abuse highlights the difficulty each of us has trying to remember childhood experiences, much less interpret them. Roseanne Arnold, the television star, claims that she remembers being abused by her mother when she was six months old. Singer LaToya Jackson alleges that she was abused as a child. In these cases siblings and parents denied the charges and claimed that the events were imaginary. Memory is a complex function, and it is very difficult to recall in adult life what really happened in childhood.

When we look back on our lives, we have choices. We can remember only the bad times and allow those moments of pain, disappointment, and rejection to define us. We can judge ourselves on the impressions of others and we can blame others for failure; or, we can take responsibility for our own lives. Although we cannot deny negative feelings, we can integrate them into our consciousness so they are reality-based. To get to the bottom of this, we need to understand why we feel and act as we do.

Adult children can have bad feelings toward parents who had nurtured different expectations for them. Because they set different goals for themselves, these children received negative feedback from their parents. Without faith in themselves, they feel alienated and hopeless. They need to remain committed to their own reality and learn to solve their own problems. If they give up and accept a state of helplessness, they will always feel rejected and dejected. The key is believing in yourself. Believe the decisions you make are valid and true. Accept your own feelings and your own reality. Don't feel that you must act to please others.

Freedom exists if you believe that you have choices. If you don't like the way you are now, accept it and plan to change. But first understand and accept the way you are; otherwise, you will always be in denial, so anxious and humiliated that you will be unable to change. Don't blame parents, friends, or the world. Accept yourself and take responsibility. Once you accept and feel good about yourself, you can accept and like others. If you are happy with your own company, you won't become dependent on others.

We are all wounded by our parents. Survivors use the wound as a source of energy, an exit from oppression and blame, and an entry to a new, separate reality. Whether the wound was inflicted by an alcoholic father, a shaming mother, abuse, or isolation, it is the fountain of the child's energy and genius. The child who soars above the wounding excels at life. Victims, on the other hand, flee from parents to brood or sulk. They are not ready to come back and make up again. These children live in shame as victims, obsessed by their wounds in a morass of self-pity and rage. They live in a fog which blurs reality and dulls awareness.

I Learned Nothing from My Father

I met Don, a very successful retired family doctor, in Tasmania. He was born in Scotland. His mother died when he was an infant and he was reared by his father, a very rich and successful businessman. His father ignored him. He hardly ever spoke to his son because Don stuttered. When his father remarried and had a second family, Don was rejected.

After the Second World War, Don came to Tasmania and lost contact with his father. He married and had three children. An excellent father, he was very close to his children and grandchildren. His family was very loving and supportive. He visited his grandchildren almost daily, and the grandchildren were devoted to him.

While Don was telling me about his father, he commented, "I never learned very much from my father, he was such a quiet man." But I think he learned a great deal. He learned from his father's mistakes. He learned how *not* to treat his children. He did not make the same mistakes his father had made with him.

Don soared above his wounds and used his energy to make himself independent and self-reliant. He was a private man with very clear boundaries; he let others get only as close to him as he wished them to be. Although Don never really knew what his father did in business, he had always assumed that he cheated people. He felt responsible for his father's actions and carried a sense of guilt because of it. In many cases we either imitate parents or take the opposite path. To make up for the wrongdoings of his father, Don became a humanitarian, a physician devoted to helping others. He accepted his father, forgave him, and got on with his life.

As hard as we may try, whether we are aware of it or not, we can't ignore our parents because we are constantly reacting to them. We use the same language, the same mannerisms, and the same problem-solving strategies. We start to sound the same, and time chisels us so we start to look the same. If we reject our parents, we are reacting to them. We can learn a great deal from our parents by taking the best of their qualities and rejecting those we don't like. But one thing we can't do is ignore them.

It's All My Father's Fault

"My father was cold. He never noticed me. He didn't acknowledge anything I did. He never showed me any affection or love. He made me feel useless and guilty all the time. I always felt rejected by him. Because of him, I have felt rejection all my life."

Many of the physical and psychological problems I deal with in the elderly result from problems that began in childhood. People who as children felt unloved, ignored, or abused by their parents may never manage to deal with the wounds. The source of the above quotation is not a juvenile charged with robbery or a hardened criminal justifying a life of crime. It is an 84-year-old man called Bernie. His father had been dead for more than thirty years, yet Bernie had never forgiven him. Like the child Franz Kafka described in "Letter to His Father," Bernie had been abused by his father over a long period of time.

Although Bernie had been a small, timid child, his father wanted to raise him to be fearless and strong. He denied Bernie the validity of his reality, and continually harped on about his own difficult childhood. When Bernie had a problem, his father mocked him: "If that's all you have to worry about, I only wish I had your problems." Once when Bernie refused to eat his dinner, his father went into a wild rage and threatened to send him to an orphanage. The fact that his parent would kick him out of the house for such a trivial thing completely undermined Bernie's self-confidence and convinced him he was worthless. After that he continually lived in fear that he would be sent to an orphanage for the smallest of transgressions.

His father had made up his mind what he wanted Bernie to do and closed every path that his son wanted to go down. When Bernie had an opinion that his father disagreed with, instead of saying "I don't agree with that idea," his father told him that he was stupid. Bernie lost the capacity to think for himself; it was safer to agree with his father all the time. He became nervous and anxious.

He lost faith in his own judgment and lived in constant dread that something catastrophic was about to take place. Completely lacking in confidence, he lived life like a thief about to be discovered, forever in fear that he would be found out and exposed for what he really was—useless.

Bernie sought every means of escape from his father and himself. He ran away from home to join the army and never returned. Over the years, from telling and retelling the stories of his childhood, he had placed an evil specter where his father should have been. He could not think of a single good thing to say about him. Nevertheless, he wished he had met his father and talked to him before his death. His need for approval and love had eaten away at him like a cancer. Bernie never recovered from his childhood wounds. When I met him, he agreed with everything I said. He admitted that he had a problem, then blamed his father. Because he repeated the same points over and over again, it was impossible to finish the conversation. He pinned people with his need, and every time I said good-bye, I felt like I was stranding him on a desert island. His insecurity and need for continual reassurance and affirmation made it difficult to be around him. If someone disagreed with him, he immediately assumed that person was criticizing him. He could not progress and stand alone because he had never resolved his problems with his father.

All parents wound their children, some more seriously than others. Children who try to ignore or avoid a bad parental relationship will always have the wound. It gnaws away at them. When life is going well, they don't seem to notice it. But when the going gets rough, they feel it and suffer. This relationship with our parents defines us as friends, lovers, and parents by forming the template for all future relationships. We need to accept these wounds and come to terms with them. They are the door to understanding and the conception of a new reality.

Do you relate to Bernie or Don? Are you a victim or a survivor? Each of us has parts of each at different times. Are you perpetuating your childhood problems in your present relationships?

There is a third type of child, who reacts to the parental wound by denying all feelings. These children are emotionally dead at the core. They will not talk about their parents and have lost contact. In the car they listen to the radio or CD, and turn on the television once they enter the house. They pick up the phone and talk for hours about nothing—certainly not their own feelings. They can do anything but sit in silence or be alone. Their lives are filled with chatter, gossip, and sensation. They constantly react to the surrounding environment and have difficulty generating feelings themselves. These men and women live on the surface of life, distracted by sensation and afraid to look inside because they might fall into the black hole and never come out.

3
Getting Started

The relationship with parents is potentially dangerous and damaging for some children. If they allow it, caring for parents can burden children with intolerable and destructive emotions and feelings of failure and inadequacy. When older parents start to fail, they often have multiple interrelated medical, personal-care, emotional, spiritual, and social problems. Children who want to help must be resourceful, flexible, and thoughtful.

Battered Children

Giuseppe and his two brothers care for their 76-year-old widowed mother, Rosa. She lives with one of the brothers in a granny flat. Giuseppe visited almost every day. His mother had had several strokes, and this caused chronic pain in her right side. She also has impaired memory and judgment and is very depressed and angry. He was burned out trying to cope with his mother's anger. Every time he visited, she complained because he "didn't visit enough," he "didn't care," he was "mean to her." No matter what he did, it wasn't good enough.

He told me his mother became frustrated when she couldn't use the phone or got mixed up. One day Rosa locked herself in her apartment and couldn't open the lock. She took a hammer to it and smashed the door. Another time, when she couldn't get a ring off her finger, she smashed her finger with a hammer. I explained that she was also hammering at him and his brothers.

Rosa's sons felt guilty because she was in pain, and because she was failing and there was only so much they could do for her.

Giuseppe felt that his own life was slipping out of control. His relationship with his mother was damaging his relationship with his wife and children. He told me, "I feel angry all the time. My oldest son told me my problem is that I can't let go. My wife says my problem is that I want to control my mother's illness and I can't let her go."

Giuseppe was being damaged by his mother's battering. She was projecting her anger and anxiety onto him and he did not know how to defend himself. He developed high blood pressure and was getting pains in his chest. I advised Giuseppe to stay involved but told him to:

- stop assuming responsibility for his mother's illness;
- distance himself emotionally from his mother to protect himself;
- park his car a block from his mother's house and walk there, taking time to center himself and take control of his emotions to prevent himself from being sucked into Rosa's depression, anger, and frustration;
- walk back to his car to "decompress" on the way and try to let go of his ambivalent feelings toward his mother.

How does Giuseppe center himself and take control before he visits his mother? There is a short focusing or centering exercise he can perform, especially when he is feeling anxious or upset. The first step is to sit comfortably, breathing in and out slowly and deeply. Next he focuses his mind on a quiet image in nature which gives him a sense of peace. If he becomes distracted, he needs to bring his mind back to that image of peace. He must not tighten up or force his mind to be still—just stay calm and intent on the image. If he is driving, he should sit back, relax his grip on the wheel, and center himself. He will feel a sense of quiet and his anxieties will drift slowly away.

It is important for Giuseppe to retain this sense of peace and control. To protect himself, he must distance himself emotionally from his mother.

He does this by first becoming aware of his own feelings. Is he anxious, angry, tired, fed up, or bored? What is his body language? Is he gripping the wheel in a tense or relaxed manner? Once he is aware of his feelings and his body language, he should breathe deeply and relax. When he goes to his mother's house, he must try to stay relaxed and not get pulled into Rosa's emotional state.

This was my "prescription" to help Giuseppe help his mother:

- *Center* yourself.
- *Diagnose* your mother's emotional state. Is she happy, sad, angry, anxious?
- *Don't take it personally*. If she is angry, sad, or anxious, don't take it on. "Turn sideways" and let it go by. When she is finished venting, take this moment to:
- *Empathize:* "I understand why you are angry. I would be angry, too. I don't blame you."
- *Reassure:* "I love you." "I want to help you." "What can I do?"
- *Make a plan:* "Together we can beat this." "Our love is stronger than the anger."
- *Follow up:* "Whatever happens, I will be here for you." "Even though I can't physically be here with you all the time because of other obligations, I will help when I can." "I will see you soon."

Angry people make us feel angry, happy people make us happy, and uptight people make us anxious, if we let them. Giuseppe needs to be aware of his own feelings and take control. When he visits his mother, he must remain intent on staying calm, monitor her behavior, and analyze it. For example, "She is smiling, happy to see me; now she is angry and complaining I don't come often enough. I must not react. Keep cool, smile, distract. I am going to stay in control." This takes time, but if he loses control, he cannot help her.

Most parents give their children shelter, love, nourishment, education, confidence, and the opportunity to grow and be happy. What does the child owe the parent? Parents deserve gratitude, respect, and love for the love and attention they have given to their children. Our parents' aging and death provide an opportunity to come to terms with and prepare for our own. We learn firsthand how to handle old age, so we will minimize the burden on our own children and friends when our time comes.

Adult Children Taking Charge

As we grow older, we live with partners who may have different sets of values and different coping mechanisms. In the workplace and from friends, we learn how to use a variety of coping skills to deal with problems. By mid-life, without even being aware of it, we have learned to deal with the different behavior patterns of other people and possess a repertoire of coping strategies.

As people mature, they gain stature and power in the family and have an opportunity to change the way it operates. Adult children can heal a dysfunctional family and make it healthy and supportive. When parents start to fail, adult children can help their mothers and fathers deal with the problems and develop solutions. Families cope in a variety of ways with aging parents. For example, children can share out the tasks to provide the range of support needed. However, it is not unusual for one child to bear most of the burden. This child will often do 90 percent of the care-giving.

Caring for older adults is not like raising a child. It's a totally different experience because older adults are not like children; they have different needs. Guilt and obligation are the worst reasons for caregiving. Many children who abuse their parents are financially or psychologically dependent on them or have been abused themselves. The best caregivers are those who care voluntarily, with a light heart.

As parents age, they become more prone to develop disabilities that impair their ability to care for themselves. This limits their independence and freedom. When this happens, someone else must fill in the gaps so they can continue to function. In many cases, a child who is usually busy trying to manage his or her own life takes on this responsibility. For many, this burden is very difficult to accept because they feel it was thrust upon them. They don't want it, but there is no one else; they feel that they have no choice in the matter. They feel stressed trying to keep their lives together while responding to the problems associated with this added responsibility.

Kate, a successful businesswoman and an only child, has returned from a business trip. When she checks her answering machine, she discovers that her mother, Rebecca, has left three messages, all roughly the same. "Hi, dear, just checking to see if you're back. I can't remember if you said Saturday or Sunday. Don't call me if you get in too late."

Rebecca lives with her husband, Doug, in a small house about twenty minutes away from their daughter's apartment. Kate calls immediately. Her mother answers the phone, sounding anxious and tired.

"Hi, Mom, I'm back. Is everything okay? Do you need any-thing?"

Rebecca replies, "Well, I'm surprised you have time to phone your old mother. What do we ever want from you, a bigshot, always traveling around while we just sit here day after day, day in and day out. It must be nice being such a celebrity."

Kate is hurt and confused. "Mom, that's not fair. I think of you and Dad all the time. I worry about you. Why are you being so mean and resentful? I feel like I'm losing my best friend. Why are you so angry with me all the time?"

"I'm sorry, dear. I'm not feeling very well today. I've had a headache all day and I didn't sleep last night."

Kate feels guilty now. "I'm sorry, Mom, can I get you anything? I'll come by tomorrow after work."

Rebecca sighs. "I have to hang up now because I feel tired, but not as tired as you must be. Good night, dear. See you tomorrow."

Kate holds the dead line in her hand. "Why is she doing this to me? Why is she so miserable to me all the time? What's happening to her? Why does she always make me feel responsible and guilty? I try to be a good daughter, I really do my best, but it seems I can never do enough. We were best friends and now she treats me like an enemy. It's almost as if she's jealous of me. What can I do?"

Most children will have these thoughts for a while after this kind of conversation, then just carry on with their lives. Some children think, "She's miserable, she's getting old, nothing can be done about it." They develop an uneasy feeling when they think about their parent and may start to resent and dread their parent's phone calls. As time goes on, they may avoid calling home and try to minimize contact with the parent. They may even blame their parent for the change in his or her behavior. They don't appreciate that it is often part of an illness or depression.

Kate has a problem, but she doesn't know what to do about it. She has three choices: She can back off, make excuses, and try to minimize contact with her mother and father. She can continue to stay involved and deal with issues as they arise from day to day. Or she can become more actively involved and try to help them.

If she chooses the first option and ignores them, she leaves them to work out their own problems. She can rationalize this by saying her parents are too stubborn, too selfish, and too independent to listen to her; her mother is emotionally abusive and places impossible demands on her; or her mother is getting old and there's nothing anybody can do about it.

Love, obligation, and/or guilt would lead Kate on a different path—to help her parents. If she cares out of obligation or duty, she will try to provide the minimum she feels is owed. First she must judge how much is owed. What kinds of parents were they? She has to roll all her experiences into a ball and weigh it in her hand. But how does she measure it? There is no yardstick, no balance. How can she really compare her life with another's? Experiences, memories, and relationships can't be objectively examined under a microscope or weighed on a scale.

When she tries to judge whether they were overprotective, neglectful, or even abusive, she has only her own experiences to guide her. When they seemed too strict, were they expressing their love by trying to protect her? When they got angry, were they trying to teach her something? When they ignored her, was it neglect or were they giving her more freedom? When they were irritable, were they exhausted from trying to earn a living and dealing with daily hassles? How do you measure a person or a lifelong relationship?

What really drives her mother? Can we ever really know ourselves, never mind another? It's not easy for children to divine parental motives and look back through the mists of time, colored by emotion, immaturity, and the child's subjective perspective as a player involved in the scenes, to judge their parents. Will Kate allow a few intense emotional scenes to influence her impressions, like a lighthouse beacon illuminating a few yards of a hundred-mile coastline? Will these few moments outweigh the rest of their lives together? How many countless hours have gone unrecorded, while a few short moments overshadow the rest?

Some children whose parents were verbally or physically abusive, addicted, selfish, or neglectful may be able to decide very quickly what they owe. Others who had wonderful, generous, loving parents will have no problems making up their minds either. Kate has to go on a gut feeling in the end. There is no simple formula such as:

$$5 \times \text{love} + 3 \times \text{guilt} + 2 \times \text{duty} =$$
$$7 \text{ phone calls} + 5 \text{ hours of care weekly}$$

In the end, Kate responds out of a mixture of guilt, love, duty, compassion, and hope. She decides that she is going to help. At the moment she is not even sure what she can do, but she must start somewhere. Once she has decided to help, she needs to approach and deal with the problems rationally. Here are the seven steps I advised her to follow:

1. Identify the problems.
2. Discuss the issues with your parent.
3. Get a proper assessment.
4. Set up a comprehensive plan.
5. Make a deal and set limits.
6. Take care of yourself and prevent burnout.
7. Continue to monitor the situation.

1. Identify the Problems

There are three parts to this issue: Rebecca, Kate, and Kate and Rebecca's relationship. Rebecca has changed. She has become resentful, angry, anxious, and miserable. Kate feels confused, guilty, hurt, angry, and sad. Their relationship has changed dramatically over the past few months. Kate considered her mother her best friend, but recently Rebecca's behavior has driven a wedge between them.

Kate is confused because she doesn't understand why Rebecca is treating her this way. There's no obvious reason for it. She needs to analyze the problem before she can come to grips with it; otherwise, she will be overwhelmed by it. Here are some simple questions to help Kate explore the issues.

When did the problem start? About nine months ago Rebecca had a mammogram for suspected breast cancer. Although the tests were negative, she started to change around that time. Shortly afterward, she changed her high-blood-pressure medication. Kate wonders if the medication could have affected Rebecca's personality. She makes a note to get Rebecca a checkup from her doctor.

Does Rebecca have problems with other family members? Rebecca has become very critical of her husband, Doug. She blames him for making poor economic decisions that have left them financially strapped and on a tight budget. She is embarrassed that they are poor, and resentful that many of their friends and relatives are better off. Rebecca doesn't go out with her sister any more. Kate makes a note to talk to Aunt Betty.

Has there been any change in her ability to function? Often, the first sign of illness in the elderly is a change in their ability to carry out the activities of daily living. Usually more complex tasks are affected first. They start to have problems with managing finances, shopping, driving, grooming, housekeeping, or cooking. Physical diseases may not have the classic physical symptoms and signs in older people. For example, many have heart attacks but don't experience any chest pain. An older adult with pneumonia may not have a cough or fever. The only outward sign may be confusion. They may even ignore physical symptoms, putting them down to "just old age." Almost 3,000 years ago, Hippocrates wrote: "In old persons the heat is feeble, and therefore they require little fuel, as it were, to the flame, for it would be extinguished by much. On this account, also, fevers in old people are not equally acute, because their bodies are cold. Old people, on the whole, have fewer complaints than young; but those chronic diseases which do befall them generally never leave."

Doug has taken over the finances, shopping, and cooking, and seems to be compensating for Rebecca. He may believe his wife's problems are just old age and inevitable, or he may not want to burden Kate with their problems.

Has there been a change in mood? Is she depressed? Depression is the great mimic. Children, and even doctors, often miss it because it can present itself in so many different ways. Older people often hide and deny emotional problems. Depression and anxiety may cause physical complaints or a change in emotional state. They may become anxious but maintain their activity level. See page 57 for further information.

Any physical changes? Has Rebecca lost weight? Does she have pain, shortness of breath, or indigestion? Physical illnesses can also cause irritability and emotional changes.

Is Kate the problem? Kate must examine her role in the relationship, how the problem affects her and her response to her mother. She needs to become aware of how this change in Rebecca's behavior makes her feel and how she reacts to it. She needs to examine why this situation is causing so much suffering. What is happening that makes her feel so bad and what can she do to deal with it?

Her mother wanted her to marry and have children. When Kate was young, Rebecca bought her pretty dresses and signed her up for ballet lessons. Kate grew up in jeans, played baseball, and wanted a baseball glove for her birthday. Rebecca was disappointed when Kate divorced. She wants grandchildren and has nagged her daughter about it for years. Perhaps her mother now realizes that this will never happen. She may believe that Kate is selfish because she never had children.

On the other hand, is her mother trying to tell Kate something? Is Kate a workaholic, pouring her life into her work because she is afraid of being hurt in relationships? Is this what Rebecca is getting at by criticizing her work habits? Is her mother using the illness to pull Kate in closer and tighten control? Does she still treat Kate as her little girl in fancy dresses and bows, or is she driving her away because she feels the end coming?

Kate needs to talk to her mother. To get a broader perspective on the issues, she also needs to talk to others in the family. At this point, she has some options:

- She can talk to her mother.
- She can talk to her father.
- She can talk to Aunt Betty, her mother's sister.

She decides not to talk to her mother just yet. First, she wants to see if her concerns are shared by others. Kate phones her father the next day.

"Hi, Dad," Kate greets him cheerfully.

"Hello, dear. How are you?" He sounds surprised.

"Fine, but I need to talk to you in private about Mom's problems. Can you talk now?"

He whispers, "It's okay, we can talk now. She's having a nap."

Kate asks, "How has Mom been lately? Have you noticed any changes?"

Doug replies a little hesitantly, "She's all right, dear. She may be slowing down a bit, but she's not getting any younger, you know; neither am I, for that matter."

"Are you doing more around the house these days? Has Mom been more irritable lately?" Kate inquires.

Doug is getting a little uncomfortable. "I guess for the past few months, I've been doing most of the housework because your mother just doesn't feel up to it. She's been feeling irritable and won't visit her doctor because she's afraid he'll find another lump. I didn't want to tell you because you're busy and I didn't want to worry you. I'm hoping it's nothing too serious. As long as it's not Alzheimer's disease, I don't mind. I don't know if I could handle that."

Kate realizes that there is a real problem with Rebecca. Her mother has changed emotionally and has deteriorated to the point where she can't do her housework. Medical problems may be at the root of this. Kate and her father decide that the next step is to arrange a proper assessment to get to the bottom of the problem. But before they do, they agree to discuss this with Rebecca.

I saw Rebecca in my clinic. She had anemia, which responded well to iron replacement. The high-blood-pressure medication was causing depression. When it was changed, she had a significant improvement in her mood, memory, and function. She slowly improved over the following months.

2. Discuss the Issues with Your Parent

This is often the most difficult part of the process for children. Parents are used to telling children what to do. Once the child recognizes that the parent is having problems, the child's relationship with the parent starts to change. As soon as the child starts to give care and make decisions for the parent, the power in the relationship shifts. This can be a very tricky transition if the parent does not acknowledge that there is a problem. Parents may not want to give up power to their children or burden them with their care. They may become angry, resentful, or even paranoid. Parents will often accuse children of being busybodies, interfering, and overstepping their authority.

You need to handle this transition with patience and tact. At times you may even need to resort to subterfuge and tell a few white lies, particularly if your parent does not acknowledge that there is a problem.

Your opening gambit is to sound out your parent to determine his or her perspective.

Andrea came home for her mother's funeral. Her father, George, an 84-year-old widower, lived alone in his own home in the country. Andrea was concerned that he was failing. He had glaucoma, which impaired his vision, and severe arthritis in the hip from an old war wound in the thigh. After the funeral, she talked to him. "Dad, I may not get a chance to see you again for some time. You are obviously getting frail and you can't stay here much longer. I want to organize everything now while I'm here. I think you should sell the house and move into a retirement home. You need to bring your will up to date now that Mom is dead. Then you should give me your power of attorney."

Her father threw her out and gave his neighbor power of attorney.

Andrea made three mistakes. First, she tried to deal with her father's problems while he was coping with his wife's death. He was not ready. Second, she did not involve him. She tried to impose her solutions on her father; she would have casually taken his freedom by conveniently packing him off to a home. Because he would be in a supervised setting, she would have nothing to worry about and her inheritance would be safe. Finally, there was no discussion; she dictated to him. I understand why George did not want his daughter involved in his care. If he became confused and had to rely on her to make decisions for him, she would put him in a home the first chance she got. How could he trust her again? This is how *not* to do it.

Jim had a different approach.

Jim first noticed that his mother, Joan, and father, Sam, were aging when his mother kept phoning him to check arrangements they had made. Sam was slowing down. Once when Jim came to take his parents out for dinner, they weren't there. They had mixed up the dates. Jim was one of five children. This is how he approached the problem.

He invited his parents out for dinner. Over dinner he broached the subject. "Mom and Dad, you know I love you very much. I don't want to interfere in your lives or tell you what to do, but I want to talk to you about something important. My friend's mother, a widow, had a stroke recently. She can't speak, and the family are in a crisis. They don't have the deeds to her house. She has a safety deposit box, but the bank won't let them into it because she hasn't signed a power of attorney. Now the family can't do anything. The government is becoming involved, and the children have to try to go before the court to become her guardians so they can manage her care. Worse still, the children can't agree, and nobody knows what decisions to make for her.

"I don't want to tell you what to do or to take over your lives, but I want to make sure I know what you want if anything should ever happen to you. First and foremost, I want to be able to do the right thing for you. I don't want the children to disagree about anything. I don't want us to feel guilty for the rest of our lives, wondering if we did the wrong thing. If we fight over what we should do, it could divide us forever. It would be bad enough losing you, but it would be a disaster if it divided the family."

Jim's approach was completely different from Andrea's. He wanted to do what his parents wanted. He was offering to help: "Have you thought about these things?" "How can I help you?" He was not telling his parents what to do. He explained what prompted him to have the conversation— the disaster in his friend's family. He appealed to them to make their wishes known to protect themselves and their children. This is a very powerful argument for any parent. He kept stressing that he wanted to know their wishes so he could do what *they* wanted. In short, he was appealing, not dictating, to them.

Jim is making a deal with his parents. He is saying, "If you tell me what you want, I will carry out your wishes. I am doing it because I love you and want the best for you.

This is an act of love, not an attempt to take control of your lives."

There are many different ways to start this conversation. One obvious way is to wait until the subject comes up, perhaps when you are talking about someone who is ill, dying, or has died. You can say, "If I ever became ill and couldn't communicate, I'd like to tell you what I want you to do for me. By the way, what would you want if this ever happened to you?" You could come right out and say, "I would like to discuss something that I have been thinking about for some time now. I want to talk to you about what you would want if you were too ill to communicate. I'd like to know so I can do everything to make sure you receive the treatment you want." The most important thing is not to coerce your parent to talk about it if he or she is not ready or willing. There are some people who, for a variety of reasons such as shyness, fear, mistrust, or denial, cannot talk about such intimate things.

If you prefer to raise the issue obliquely, rent a movie about illness and death and use it as an opening for discussion. This conversation can be extended to include care in the home, nursing homes, funeral arrangements, and method of burial. Most parents have thought about these issues but may feel their children are not ready to discuss them. Other parents do not want to burden their children. Many are delighted to discuss their wishes; however, children often back away from the subject because they find it too morbid.

If Jim is rebuffed, he should not try to push the issue. Either Joan and Sam have not thought about the issue, or they have and don't want to give him the responsibility. Before talking to his parents, he might want to discuss the issue with his brothers and sisters to find out if any of them have financial power of attorney or have discussed their parents' wishes with them. If another child has power of attorney, then it is obvious that his parents do not want Jim to handle their financial affairs.

If none of the children has been informed of Joan and Sam's wishes, or if the couple have not assigned a power of attorney, then Jim may want to ask a brother or sister, or one of his parents' friends, to begin this conversation. He could also try again himself by giving his parents a copy of an advance directive (a living will or medical directive) to open this conversation (see page 183).

The main purpose of this conversation is to establish what parents want, to find out what their thinking is on these issues. You might use a leading question such as, "If you had a stroke that paralyzed you so that you could not walk or talk, would you want to be kept alive on machines?" Continually emphasize that you want to know so you can do what they want. If a parent is resisting attempts to discuss these issues, book an appointment with the family doctor to discuss your problems. Parents may be more receptive to authority figures than to their children. You could also recruit a minister or priest, a close friend, or another person your parents respect and trust to encourage them to make plans.

Gilles can beg, plead, or implore, but he should never coerce or force his parents to make these decisions. Some people have great difficulty coming to terms with their own mortality. They may have magical thinking: "If I don't think about this, it will never happen." Or they just don't want to deal with it. If that's the case, Gilles may want to start discussing these issues with his brothers and sisters so at least they have started thinking about it and will have a plan if something does happen suddenly.

In families each sibling can have a different relationship with the parents. One child may be able to have this conversation, whereas another may fail. If his parents discuss these issues with Gilles, all of the children should be informed of the parents' wishes. Treating these decisions as secrets is a recipe for discontent and acrimony because the other siblings may feel excluded. If at all possible, parents should write down their wishes and be as clear and explicit as possible. Even if one child is given power of attorney, all the others should be informed about it; otherwise the children who have been excluded may harbor suspicions that the parents were coerced or that their wishes have been misconstrued.

3. Get a Proper Assessment

Since medical conditions such as arthritis, anemia, and vision or hearing problems can compromise an older person's ability to function independently, any assessment of an elder must include not only a medical examination, but also a comprehensive evaluation of his or her physical and mental ability, illnesses, disabilities, handicaps, and resources. All of these determine the elder's ability to function in his or her own setting. The assessment looks at the total person in a holistic fashion to determine strengths as well as problems. In addition to a careful physical examination, the elder should have a home assessment. Geriatric assessment is usually performed by a team of health professionals which includes a trained geriatrician (a doctor specializing in the care of older adults), geriatric nurse specialists, physiotherapists, occupational therapists, social workers, and even chaplains. In a proper assessment, the following are covered:

- physical health (nourishment, angina, diabetes, arthritis, blindness, deafness, etc.);
- mental health (memory loss, depression);
- environment (safety; getting around; impediments to independence; risk of tripping, falling, or burns);
- social supports (family network, friends, church, and others);
- coping mechanism (level of adaptation to disability and other problems);
- assessment in the home.

The home assessment is an integral part of the overall assessment of frail older adults. There is no substitute for observing elders groping their way through a cluttered, dark living room; wobbling around sharp edges of shaky furniture; climbing a rickety footstool to reach the top shelf in the kitchen; shuffling over loose rugs on uneven, slippery floors; and climbing up or down loose, creaking stairs. Clinic examinations just don't provide this type of information. There is no better clue than an empty fridge to account for weight loss or a box full of beer or wine empties to account for "confusion and falls." Problems like wandering, unsafe driving, hazardous bathing habits, or unsafe performance of household tasks are often missed in the doctor's office. Other problems that are picked up at home include loneliness, lack of socialization, confusion, family stress, inappropriate medications, poor vision, incontinence, and poor hygiene.

An occupational therapist, or nurse, usually does the home assessment. She can recommend aids—seats in the shower or grab bars in the bathroom. She can tape the stairs to outline the steps and make some suggestions about lighting and the removal of scatter rugs. As well, she can suggest many different ways to improve safety and increase independence.

Social workers discuss day centers, activity programs, and assisted transportation. Chaplains discuss spiritual issues, even emotional problems stemming from guilt, fears, or regrets. They may provide tremendous comfort and peace.

4. Set Up a Comprehensive Plan

Richard and Ann lived alone in their small home. They were a devoted couple. Richard had a heart attack and was admitted to hospital. When their daughter, Nancy, came to visit from out of town, she was horrified to find that Ann was completely unable

to cope. Her mother was confused and thought Richard had gone
shopping. She couldn't cook and the house was a mess. Ann had
urine stains on her dress, was very anxious, and kept asking
Nancy when Richard would be coming back. Nancy kept telling
her he was in the hospital, but this just made her mother more
upset. Later, she found Ann's thyroid and high-blood-pressure
pills mixed together in the same container.

Richard had been covering for his wife for the last few
years. He had gradually taken over the cooking and cleaning. Nancy and the rest of the family never really appreciated how dependent Ann was on him. He filled in for her,
shielded her, and had managed to fool everyone.

Faced with an ill father and confused mother, Nancy
becomes very anxious and then panics. Her first reaction is
emotional, which blurs reality and objectivity. She must
stop reacting and start responding by stepping back from
the situation and looking at it clearly and objectively. Her
mother is confused. It may not be possible to change that.
Nancy must come to terms with her mother's situation,
cope with her own feelings, understand Ann's problem,
and develop a strategy to deal with it. Once she starts to
take stock of the situation, she will begin to gain some
understanding and control. She can't leave Ann alone. Can
she take her home to stay with her until she gets some
help?

Nancy's mother has physical, functional, emotional, and
social needs. The family must make a plan for the future.
Ann is probably not competent and can't make decisions
for herself. Competent people understand their own situation and appreciate the choices available to them and the
likely consequences of those choices. Because Ann has such
severe memory loss that she cannot even appreciate that
her husband is in the hospital, it is very unlikely that she
can make rational choices for herself.

Richard, however, is competent and is responsible for
his wife's care. He has the authority to make decisions for

her. But his hospitalization means that it is Nancy who must act. Any choice that she makes for her mother must take into account Ann's values, dignity, and goals. In other words, Nancy should do what she thinks her mother would do in these circumstances. If she does not know what her mother would do, then she must do what is best for Ann.

The areas that need to be covered are:

Physical needs Her mother's medical conditions need attention. She may have taken too many or too few thyroid or blood-pressure pills. Her blood pressure may be out of control, or she may even have had a mild stroke, which would account for the sudden loss of memory. This should be checked. Other physical needs might include arthritis relief, pain management, dressings, and vision or hearing aids.

Functional needs These include two categories: Instrumental Activities of Daily Living (IADL) and Basic Activities of Daily Living (BADL). Instrumental activities include complex tasks such as driving, managing medications, handling finances, shopping, cooking, and cleaning. Basic activities include simple tasks such as walking, washing, dressing, grooming, toileting, and feeding.

Ann cannot manage instrumental activities and has difficulty with some basic activities. She cannot live alone. The family may want to modify the home to ensure her safety and independence. She may need to live with Nancy. Nancy may have to stay with her mother or hire someone to take care of her. Or Ann may need to go into an institution. But before any of these decisions are made, she should have a checkup by a doctor.

Nancy will have to wait and see how her father progresses. In the end, Ann's care will be Richard's decision. It would be premature to make permanent decisions about it at this point. Nancy could, however, place her mother in a nursing home for a short stay. Respite care provides short-term accommodation, from weeks to months, in a nursing home (see page 166).

What if Ann deteriorates further so that she doesn't recognize family members, loses control of her bowels and bladder, and can't walk? What if she doesn't recover? Nancy needs to complete applications for nursing homes now.

Emotional needs Ann needs emotional support. She needs to be reassured that she will be taken care of. She needs to be able to talk about her concerns and feel that her family understands and supports her. If she becomes anxious or depressed, she may become irritable. Even if she has had a stroke or suffers from Alzheimer's, which robs her of her ability to communicate, Nancy can still communicate with her. She can communicate with touch, smiling, and listening, and by doing simple tasks together.

Social needs Ann needs to stay connected with her church, friends, family, organizations, and neighbors as much as possible. Family members should help her maintain and nurture these connections.

When Ann was taken to the doctor, he checked her blood pressure and found it was high. He also did blood tests to check her thyroid function. Nancy has been with her mother for four days now and is getting tired. She is having a hard time keeping up with her mother's demands and is up off and on all night because Ann doesn't sleep well. At the same time she feels guilty because she has left her own family and her work.

Nancy assured her father that she will take care of Ann until he is discharged. The doctors have told Nancy that the stress of caring for his wife may be too much for Richard. They are concerned about letting him go back home so soon after a heart attack. At this point Nancy must decide what her long-term involvement will be. She is being forced to make decisions.

Nancy can't be expected to sacrifice her emotional or physical health for her mother. Many children become exhausted, burned out, and even physically ill if they try to do it all alone. Nancy is beginning to realize that she may have to put her mother in a nursing home or take her home to her own house. She lives in a three-bedroom house with her husband and two teenage daughters. If her mother comes to stay, she would have to put two children in one bedroom or set up a bedroom for her mother in the main living/television room. She phones home to ask her husband and her children what they think about Granny moving in. They reply that if it's necessary for a short time, they would go along with it. Her family may not want to tell her if they think it's a bad idea. They recognize that she is trapped.

There are a number of good reasons why Nancy should not take her mother home. First, there's no room for her. It's not easy for two teenagers to share a room. If they give Granny the living room, they lose the main family room in the house. If Ann goes to bed early, the children will not be able to stay up, and the family routine is disrupted. The lights go out and the house closes down. After any move, Ann is likely to become even more confused. She may want to go home all the time, and if she starts getting up in the middle of the night, looking for the bathroom or her husband, she will disrupt the household. If Nancy's husband and children feel that they cannot object, this will cause serious stress in the family. Nancy's first obligation is to her husband and children.

My advice to Nancy would be not to take her mother in. I have seen this type of arrangement seriously disrupt and damage families. If she insists on taking her mother to live with her, she needs to have an end-point. Often, when a parent comes to live with children there is no agreement or plan about what will happen when she deteriorates and her care becomes too heavy. Nursing-home placement is sought in an emergency situation.

About two-thirds of the population will spend some time in a chronic-care institution. Very few plan for this or discuss it. But they should—it's a reality for many. People who say "never put me in a nursing home" place a heavy burden on their children. Sometimes there is just no other option.

5. Make a Deal and Set Limits

Joe, an 89-year-old widower, was being placed in a nursing home after living with his daughter and son-in-law for ten years. When we finally made the decision, I asked the children what was the most difficult issue for them. His daughter spoke without any hesitation: "If I had one thing to tell other children dealing with their elderly parents, it's to set limits. You have to know when it's time to let go. We waited too long and it nearly ruined our health and our marriage."

When parents start to fail, children often jump in feet first; before they know it, they are being pulled down and they have no escape hatch. They become exhausted and entangled in obligation, guilt, love, resentment, fear, and stress because they don't know when to stop.

Any care plan must set limits. Children must decide what their time, energy, and financial limits are before they get involved. They need to make a contract with themselves, their partners, their children, their parents, and other caregivers. If possible, they need to state how far they are prepared to go in providing emotional, physical, and financial support. This helps the family decide when they need more help in the home and when it's time to look at alternative living arrangements. This is an important planning step. Without a destination, the journey never ends.

Children caring for aging parents have difficulty drawing boundaries, trying to decide what is reasonable or when the requirements are too heavy and damaging. One of the reasons for this is that love is unconditional and we may feel that our debt to our parents can't be measured. We feel overwhelmed and guilty because, no matter what we do, it will never be enough. As a result, children can just back away and do nothing, because without limits, what care they give will never be sufficient.

If at all possible, discuss this issue with partners, children, siblings, and parents. Tell them how you feel and that, although you want to do everything you can for your parents, you have limited time and resources. This is one way to get started. Decide how often you are going to call or visit. This establishes an expectation and sets some ground rules.

Sarah is a pleasant, big-hearted woman in her fifties who had married late in life. She has no children. Her husband, Peter, has severe angina, heart failure, and chronic bronchitis. He is on a disability pension and is very dependent on her. Her parents live thirty miles away. Her father, Charles, has Alzheimer's and her mother, Evelyn, is severely disabled from arthritis, cataracts, and diabetes.

Charles and Evelyn were having great difficulty coping at home. Sarah drove to their house at least two nights during the week and once on the weekends. She shopped, cooked, and cleaned for both houses. She came to see me because I was treating her father. Her face was flushed, she looked exhausted, and she was very anxious and nervous. When I asked her how she was managing, she burst into tears.

Sarah is doing everything possible to keep her parents out of a nursing home. She said they had made her promise that she would never put them in a home. At work, she spends her days worrying about her husband and parents. She never knows if she is going to come home and find Peter dead. He resents her trips to her parents. When she is at her parents' house, she feels she should be at home. When she is at home, she feels guilty about not being at her parents' house.

Sarah's two brothers, Jacob and Mark, and sister, Ruth, are too busy to help. They call their parents once a week and visit on birthdays and holidays.

One of the biggest problems faced by Sarah is her inability to draw boundaries, to answer the question: "How much do I owe my parents, how much is enough?" At the moment Sarah is sacrificing her own happiness and is beginning to resent her husband and her parents. She has no time to herself and has some of the classic features of burnout. She told me:

- She was the only one carrying the burden of care.
- She felt that she had lost control of her life.
- She felt that no matter what she did, she just couldn't satisfy all of their demands.
- She felt tired and guilty all the time.
- She felt angry a lot of the time.
- She felt helpless and overwhelmed.
- She wanted to get as far away as possible.
- She resented being near her parents.
- She felt she couldn't get away from them.
- She was not able to relax.
- She could not get them out of her mind.
- She felt depressed and hopeless.
- She had problems with sleeping, eating, and loss of energy.
- She was developing physical problems.
- She felt they were making unreasonable demands on her.

The first thing Sarah needs to do is to recognize that she must make changes. Even though she feels that it's not possible to change her situation, there is much that she can do.

Sarah has to give up some responsibility and get help. In many cases, a nursing home is the only choice. Any care plan for an elderly person must include the circumstances under which nursing-home care is an option. When someone says, "I never want to go to a nursing home," I ask, "What if you can't recognize your own family members? What if you lose control over your bowels and bladder? What if you have to be lifted in and out of bed? Do you really think it's fair to saddle your children with this burden?"

Parents have an obligation to plan for their future. Children have their own lives to live and they should not be burdened unnecessarily with decisions that are a parent's to make. Parents should consider their own

- legal and financial planning (will, power of attorney);
- medical care in the event of incompetence (advance directives, i.e., living wills);
- institutionalization and death.

To develop a clear, comprehensive plan, Sarah needs to arrange a family meeting. At the meeting, the family need to define the problem as clearly as possible, describe potential solutions and goals, and plan for a variety of different outcomes.

Sarah's Family Meeting A family conference is used for several reasons. First, it allows the family members to ask questions and receive information. Based on this information, they can then define their problems. A plan is developed, and different tasks are delegated to the family members. In short, a family meeting allows a family to organize a plan that delegates responsibility.

The fuel that keeps a family functioning is communication, and not too many of us have mastered it. At family conferences I observe how the family communicates. Who are the leaders? Who will become involved? There are usually a series of these meetings with different participants, depending on the issues discussed, but there is always a core membership who take primary responsibility for care.

At Sarah's family meeting, Sarah, her husband, her parents, and her brothers and sister attended. The first thing I did was ask them what they wanted to discuss and if they had any questions. I wanted them to talk freely about their concerns.

It's useful to develop an agenda before starting in order to keep on track. Family meetings often get out of control. Or if family members are not comfortable discussing their feelings openly, a conspiracy of silence develops around the sick. This makes parents feel more isolated and alone. We can often heal one another simply by sharing fears and concerns. Participants should be encouraged to talk freely and support each other.

After answering Sarah's family's questions, I laid out an agenda.for discussion The agenda included these items:

- their parents' medical problems
- their parents' functional problems (shopping, transport, cooking, etc.)
- psychosocial problems (anxiety, isolation, etc.)
- help they have available and help they need
- delegation of tasks to different family members
- defining the limits and end-point of the plan

Medical problems I listed both parents' medical problems and how this was leading to functional problems and psychosocial problems from anxiety and isolation.

Functional problems We listed the areas where they required help. They needed help with shopping, managing finances, cooking, transport, arranging medications, and housework. Sarah was trying to do everything herself. Her brothers and sister offered to take the finances and shopping in hand. We arranged for a visiting homemaker and Meals-on-Wheels, as well as a nurse to come in once a week to check their parents' blood pressure and blood sugars and lay out medications in a dispenser. A home-care case manager arranged these services.

Psychosocial problems We arranged for Charles and Evelyn to get assisted transportation for disabled and elderly people who cannot drive or take public transport. By going out to a seniors center on a weekly basis, they would be able to join a group of seniors and enjoy the social interaction.

Define the help they have and the help they need We discussed who wanted to lead, who would provide support, and who would take responsibility for the different tasks. We tried to reach a consensus on all points wherever possible. As we talked about the present care plan, it became obvious that Sarah was providing the bulk of the care. Her parents had refused home care and other community resources. We told them that Sarah could not keep it up any more. The other children had no idea Sarah was doing so much. It was easier for me to tell them than for Sarah to do so. From her it would have sounded like whining. From a doctor it was more acceptable.

Delegate the tasks All the children offered to help. Some had more to give than others. Those who lived farthest away agreed to phone and take time off and come to visit more often. Each of the children took responsibility for different tasks. One would always take her parents to the doctor; another would organize their banking. Yet another agreed to arrange the community resources.

Older grandchildren can take on some of these tasks, but, if at all possible, it is preferable not to force them to help. Older adults frequently have a very different relationship with their grandchildren than with their children. Grandchildren often provide a very important role simply by visiting and talking to their grandparents. They should be encouraged to visit and provide social stimulation. If they want to help with care, treat their offer as an added bonus.

Define end-points and limits It is clear that Sarah's parents are failing. Although we were able to maintain them at home using the children and community supports, they are at risk of an accident or from further deterioration. We discussed the possibility that they would deteriorate further. This would mean that one or both of them might need to live in a nursing home in the future. Charles and Evelyn have good pensions and could get capital from the sale of their house. They agreed to look at retirement homes where they could share a room. Sarah agreed to take them.

All of the children agreed that they would give the present plan a chance for a month or so. We put a communication book and a large calendar in their home. Children and professional caregivers left notes to each other. On the calendar they wrote doctor's visits, trips, and when they planned to take their parents out. This way each child could plan and ensure that there was as little overlap as possible.

Bickering families get in the way of a care plan. I always ask families to postpone their fights and come together for their parents' sake. It's also wise to allow older adults to do as much as they can for themselves. Even if they take more time and don't do a neat job, it's important to try to maintain their independence as much as possible. It's a delicate balance between doing too much or too little. It requires patience and understanding because older adults' abilities can change from day to day.

We discussed long-term planning. Charles and Evelyn have a will and a power of attorney for finances, property, health care, and personal care. We gave them an advance directive (living will) and discussed it with them. They each planned to fill one out. The group agreed to meet at least once every three months to update their plan and provide support for each other.

6. Take Care of Yourself and Prevent Burnout

Sarah needs to go easy on herself. She can't stop her parents from aging and dying. She can't let the role of caregiver swamp her other roles. It is important to keep them distinct. She can't neglect herself or her husband. The more outside help her parents have, the more time Sarah will have to spend quality time visiting. Children should justify community services for parents by saying, "I know I can do it and I would love to do it, but I don't have enough time. If we get a homemaker, I will have more time to spend with you doing the things we like doing, not just cooking and cleaning. We can enjoy each other's company."

Sarah will start experiencing anticipatory grieving—what it will be like when her parents are dead. This is normal. Sometimes at the end of a long, debilitating illness children and spouses feel relief when a parent dies. They have already done their mourning and grieving. They may even feel embarrassed because their initial relief leads to a sense of happiness. Their work is done. This is also completely normal.

Sarah needs to recognize that there will be sad times and anxious times. These are the "doldrum days" when nothing makes sense, nothing has meaning. She can't gloss over the sadness and feelings of loss. They are valid emotions and have a place in the whole process.

If her parents feel down, she should accept this and say, "I understand why you feel this way." There are some things she can't change and she can't fix. At times all she will be able to say is "I will always love you," and all she can do is listen. At other times just holding hands, hugging, or looking into their eyes is all she can give. When she stops trying too hard, or trying to change everything, it will be much easier for everyone.

Sometimes she may just need to be alone and cry. She needs to switch off the TV or the radio, take the phone off the hook, and take time alone to tune into her feelings. This is what is meant by "working through" the grief.

7. Continue to Monitor the Situation

Ideally, once the plan has been made and all the parties agree, everything should run smoothly. This almost never happens, because problems continue to arise. The key to weathering these storms is patience and perseverance. Family members need to communicate and trust each other. In making plans, it's better to involve all members of the family. It is also advisable, if problems are anticipated in the family, to have a health professional witness the agreements and keep track of progress. If there are misunderstandings later, the health professional can provide advice and keep the plan on track. These situations are emotionally laden and can be explosive and very destructive. Honesty and good communication are essential to keep everything on track.

Elder Abuse

Margaret, an only child, lived with her mother all her life. They were best friends. When Margaret's mother, Phyllis, developed Alzheimer's disease, Margaret believed she owed it to her mom to take care of her for the rest of her life. She refused to put her in a nursing home. Margaret cared for Phyllis day in and day out, all by herself.

As her condition worsened, Phyllis started saying things that hurt Margaret. Over time, she began losing control of her faculties. Margaret kept telling herself she didn't need help. One day when Phyllis was saying thoughtless things, Margaret began to call her names, tell her she didn't love her any more, and warn her that if she didn't stop being verbally abusive, she would put her into a nursing home.

Later that month, nearly five years after taking on full-time responsibility for the care of her mom, Margaret had just finished changing Phyllis's adult diaper. She wheeled her into the kitchen, where she was cooking supper. Pots were boiling over because Phyllis had been uncooperative during the diaper change and it had taken longer than usual. Just as Margaret was dealing with the chaos of dinner, Phyllis soiled herself. Margaret "lost it." She hit her mother in the face over and over. Then she started crying hysterically.

Elder abuse includes such acts as physical violence, sexual assault, neglect, insults and threats, and the misuse of an older person's money or property. The most frequent forms of abuse are psychological abuse (insults and threats), neglect (failure to provide proper care and nourishment), and financial exploitation.

It is estimated that 4 percent of the elderly population in the United States are victims of abuse in domestic settings. Usually, the victims are women, and the perpetrators are female relatives, often the caregivers. About one-quarter of elder-abuse victims are men. Elder abuse occurs in all socioeconomic levels and in all ethnic groups.

Abuse of older people can take many forms. It can be spousal abuse, where the spouse has been a victim of domestic violence in younger years and the relationship continues into old age. Elder abuse can be reversed child abuse, where a child who was abused learns abusive behavior in the home, and then uses the same violent methods to relate to an older and dependent parent. Abuse can stem from the drug abuse, mental illness, or psychopathology of the abuser, or from an economically stressed caregiver who uses the elder's money to meet his or her own financial obligations. Margaret is an example of an abuser whose caregiving stress reached such a level that she unintentionally lashed out at her mother. She did not know where to turn, and was saying and doing things to her parent that she didn't mean.

Where to Go for Help

In the United States, most states have laws and programs for handling reports of elder abuse. If you feel you are

about to lose control and become violent, or even psychologically abusive to an older person for whom you are caring, call somebody. If you don't know where to call, start
with the local social-services office. Ask to speak to a social
worker and he or she will tell you where you can turn for
help. Usually there is an elder-abuse hotline number they
will give you to call. After calling the number, you will likely receive a visit from an elder-abuse worker (also called an
adult protective-services worker). These workers are obliged to keep the report and any information obtained during
the visit confidential.

After hearing about the problem, the APS worker will
usually establish a plan for reducing the abuse risk. Often
this involves getting help with caregiving, or bringing in
more resources. The worker will provide names of agencies or support groups that can be accessed for more help
with the problem. Only when the abuse is determined to be
wilfully and maliciously perpetrated would the police be
brought in, or legal actions taken against the abuser.

4
Staying Healthy in Old Age

When patients ask me what they should do to stay healthy in old age, I have no hesitation in answering: "Keep active, eat a well-balanced diet and keep your body at or just below your ideal weight, develop a positive attitude, and try to enjoy life no matter what it throws at you. Prepare for the worst and you will never be disappointed. Take care of those who love you and never lose a sense of gratitude for life."

In developed countries, people aged 65 can now expect to live, on average, another sixteen years. Women will, on average, live for almost nineteen more years, and men about fifteen more years. At age 65, people have about twelve years of healthy living remaining and four years of disability during which they will need assistance with the basic activities of daily living, such as washing, dressing, grooming, or walking. While some think that health problems in old age are inevitable, many can be prevented or minimized.

Good health comes from reducing unnecessary suffering, illness, and disability. It comes from an improved quality of life and is measured by a person's sense of well-being. It means preventing premature death and disability, and ensuring that each person achieves and maintains a maximum level of functioning. More than anything else, people's lifestyle decisions and personal choices in a social context have a powerful influence over their health.

The most common causes of death in elders are heart disease, cancer, stroke, chronic bronchitis, pneumonia, and influenza. Although arthritis, osteoporosis, visual and hearing impairment, and dementia are not usually fatal, they often cause significant disability. It is important for older adults to develop a lifestyle that as much as possible promotes health and independence and prevents disability. If problems occur, they need to adapt to them to maintain as much independence and freedom as possible. There is growing evidence that changing behavior—even in old age—can benefit health, improve quality of life, and add years of healthy living.

The Elixir of Life

There is no secret to long life, but there are certain ingredients that increase a person's chances of health and happiness in old age. A long, healthy life is no accident for those who achieve it. People who live a simple, active life, and have a positive attitude and are optimistic, generally outlast everyone else.

The very elderly share particular lifestyles and work habits. The people I see who live to be 90 and older never smoked or drank excessively. Many are healthy, independent, and enjoying life. Those who remain healthy, involved, and connected claim that old age is the best time of their lives. More than 90 percent of the elderly live independently in their own homes, and sexual function continues into extreme old age.

Old age offers opportunity and freedom for travel, personal growth, knowledge, judgment. and wisdom. Many studies have shown that the healthy elderly are the happiest and most fulfilled group in society. Many children being born today can expect to live to more than 100. In fact, it is expected that, early in the next century, almost 2 million North Americans will be aged over 100 at any one time. There is no single formula or proven way to guarantee a long, healthy, and happy old age, but some personal choices will increase your chances.

An important factor predicting the length of a person's life is the life span of their parents. Those whose parents lived into old age are more likely to live longer. Those whose parents died in middle age from illness should be aware of any risk factors and avoid them. For example, men and women who have a family history of heart disease should eat a high-roughage, low-fat diet, have their blood pressure and cholesterol checked regularly, avoid obesity, maintain an active lifestyle, minimize stress, and never smoke.

More and more evidence is mounting that activity, even in extreme old age, can improve muscle strength. mood, sense of well-being, balance, walking, stability, bone strength, and heart and liver function. Society is slowly coming to a greater acceptance of natural aging and beginning to develop a more realistic view of old age. Many of the false myths and horror stories about aging are being shattered by healthy, active seniors in our society.

Keep Active

Activity is key to extending life and promoting and maintaining health in old age. In the past, people walked everywhere and did more physical labor. Now, technical devices save time and make life easier, but they have made us more sedentary. Because we watch television and drive everywhere, we have dramatically cut down our activity levels.

The decline in strength and function experienced by many of my patients is caused, not by aging, but by inactivity. More than 40 percent of people over 65 have no leisure-time physical activity. Fewer than a third have moderate physical activity such as walking or gardening. Fewer than 10 percent routinely engage in vigorous physical activity. Increased physical activity reduces the risk of heart disease, strokes, high blood pressure, diabetes, colon cancer, depression, and anxiety in older adults. Regular physical activity increases bone strength, reduces osteoporotic fractures, maintains body weight, and increases longevity. Middle and old age is a time to keep active and fit. Regular activity strengthens bones, exercises the heart muscle, builds endurance, improves mood and memory, and lowers cholesterol. It also improves balance, coordination, and strength, and reduces the likelihood of falls. Middle-aged and older adults can delay disability and enjoy many positive health benefits just by increasing their level of activity.

Let's remove the word "retirement" from use. It suggests to the elderly that they should take it easy. This gives the wrong message. They should keep active, busy, and fit. Old age is a time for rediscovery, renaissance, self-actualization, exploration, reflection, and renewal. It is a challenging "new age" offering enormous opportunity for growth and fulfillment.

If you or your parents plan to start an activity program or increase your activity level, discuss this with your doctor to find out if there are any special precautions you may need to take. When planning an exercise program, start off slowly, and gradually build tolerance. Exercise until you are tired but not exhausted. If you develop dizziness, shortness of breath, chest pain, or weakness, stop and seek advice. Keeping active may be the single most important thing you and your parents can do to slow the aging process.

Consider the type of activity best suited to your needs, ability, and preference. If you have arthritis of the hips, swimming or riding a bike may be better than walking, which could aggravate the problem. If you are a diabetic, you may have to take special precautions by wearing special footwear, changing medications, or changing diet. Wearing good walking shoes is important if you are walking for activity. They are expensive, but the wrong shoes can seriously damage your feet, your joints, and your back.

At the start of an activity program, exercise once a day for about fifteen minutes. Stop if you experience shortness of breath, pain, weakness, or palpitations. Take it easy and build up speed and endurance gradually. Try a variety of activities until you find one you like. There's no such thing as bad activity, unless you are straining or exercising too strenuously. You can keep fit walking in a mall or up and down corridors in an apartment building, swimming, riding a bike, dancing, bowling, curling, or golfing. If you feel silly exercising just for the sake of exercising, then try raking, mowing, sweeping, gardening, shopping, or even vacuuming. Join a community activity program like the YMCA or YWCA, a seniors activity center, or a community recreation center. It's a fun way to meet people and stay active at the same time.

To become fit, or maintain fitness, exercise for a minimum of twenty minutes, three times weekly. Those with medical problems who decide to take up an activity should get advice from a doctor, physiotherapist, or exercise physiologist. Be creative in the type of activity you choose; make it fun and enjoyable.

Vaccinations

The reduction in the incidence of infectious diseases is one of the most significant public-health achievements in this century. Nevertheless, infectious diseases still cause many preventable illnesses and deaths. Influenza and pneumonia shorten the lives of many older adults in spite of the fact that vaccinations are available to prevent them. About 90 percent of all influenza and associated deaths occur in people aged 65 or more.

Older adults need regular health care to maintain health and prevent disabling and life-threatening diseases and conditions. They should have clinical assessments to:

- detect and control high blood pressure;
- screen for high cholesterol;
- screen for cancer (for example, regular skin screening for cancer detects the majority of skin cancers);
- immunize against pneumonia and influenza;
- promote healthy behavior;
- develop a care plan to manage chronic conditions like arthritis, incontinence, and osteoporosis.

Older adults need influenza vaccines every year. Influenza ("flu") is an acute viral illness that causes sore throat, cough, fever, and generalized aches and pains. The most serious complication, pneumonia, is the fourth leading cause of death among the elderly. Immunization against influenza is a basic preventive measure for all older adults. During a flu epidemic, older adults have 30 to 100 times the death rate of younger adults. Every person aged 65 or more should receive the vaccine, but it is particularly important that elders with lung disease or other chronic illnesses receive it. The best time to get it is in October or November. This ensures that antibodies that protect against influenza are present throughout the flu season, which usually ends in March. The vaccine lasts for about one year.

The influenza vaccine is very safe. Although not all those who receive it are protected completely by it, influenza is often less severe and complications less serious in those who have been vaccinated. People who are allergic to eggs should not receive it. Side effects are rare; the most frequent side effect is soreness at the injection site for up to two days.

Pneumoccal vaccine is about 60 percent effective in protecting against pneumonia caused by the bacterium *Streptococcus pneumonia*. It cannot cause pneumonia, and side effects are similar to those experienced with influenza vaccine. It is recommended for all persons aged 65 or more, and particularly for those with lung, liver, or heart disease, cancer, or diabetes. Unlike the influenza vaccine, which is given every year, this vaccine is given only once. At present, only about 10 percent of older adults in the community receive the pneumoccal vaccine and 20 percent receive the influenza vaccine.

Diet

Certain eating habits, particularly excessive-fat and low-roughage consumption, are linked to a higher risk of heart disease, gall-bladder disease, and breast and colon cancer. In North America, dietary fat accounts for more than 35 percent of total calories, although the recommended proportion is less than 30 percent. Many North Americans are overweight, a problem associated with high blood pressure, heart disease, diabetes, high cholesterol, stroke, cancer, and gall-bladder disease.

Lean and wiry people who are active and don't overdose on calories are healthier and live longer. People get heavier as they age, mainly because of reduced activity.

Animals live longer with dietary restrictions. Compared with those that eat as much as they wish, they live 25 percent longer. They act younger, and aging diseases such as heart and kidney disease, immune-system problems, and cancer occur later. Many of these life-extending effects can be achieved even when diet restriction starts in late middle age.

I visited Okinawa, a Japanese island, to see for myself the longest-living society on earth. The islanders eat high-quality diets which are lower in calories than the diets of the mainland Japanese. The average life expectancy of Okinawans is 82 for women and 76 for men. This is a year more than the rest of Japan, which already has the highest life expectancy on the planet.

Okinawa is a two-hour flight south from the mainland over thousands of small tropical islands in a floating blue world of water and sky. Okinawans grow tropical fruit, sugar cane, and tropical flowers; eat lots of fish and seaweed; and enjoy a brisk tourist trade. I was met at the airport by some relaxed and smiling physicians who didn't have business cards. We all piled into an old rusted Nissan and drove to the capital, Naha. As we were approaching the city, I noticed some peculiar old buildings and asked what they were. I was told they were tombs and, when I expressed interest in seeing them, the driver stopped the car in the middle of a four-lane highway and we went visiting. No one stood on their horns, not one gave us the finger—other drivers just smiled and drove around our car. They could see we were visitors.

The tombs were massive and scattered over the hillside. They are shaped like a woman's womb: we come from the womb and we return to the earth's womb. After a few years in the tombs, the deceased's bones are removed by relatives, washed, and returned. There are many ceremonies connecting the present generations to their ancestors. Death is a reality Okinawans accept and do not fear.

Okinawans eat a diet low in calories but high in protein. Their excellent food consists of many small dishes of fish, seaweed, vegetables, fruit, poultry, and pork. The quality and variety is superb. They have a much lower incidence and later onset of the diseases of aging.

Dietary restriction may actually slow the clock of aging in humans. Here are some suggestions. Eat a variety of foods, with plenty of vegetables, fruit, and grains. Use sugar, salt, and alcohol in moderation. Eat a low-fat diet: remember that fat has almost double the calories per unit weight as carbohydrates and protein. However, some people with high cholesterol levels may not gain any advantage by restricting dietary fat; if you or your parent falls into this category, check with your doctor. Don't eat too much. People who live long, healthy lives have been, for the most part, light eaters.

Nearly a third of North American women and half of North American men are overweight. Keep your weight at the level that is normal for your age and body size. Dieting and then overeating carries a great risk of heart disease. The key is to develop healthy eating habits rather than using fad diets or trying to lose weight quickly. Almost 95 percent of people who lose weight quickly through diets will gain it all back within five years. Changes in basic eating habits should be made slowly. Regular activity; diets low in fats, sugars, and processed food; and good basic eating habits (eating regular meals and limiting snacking) offer the best chance for health and long life. The lesson: eat right, keep active, and you'll be a lot healthier—and happier.

Cigarettes and Alcohol

The single greatest preventable cause of death in society today is smoking. It causes one in six deaths. Cigarette smoking is responsible for about 20 percent of all deaths from heart disease, 30 percent of all cancer deaths, and almost 90 percent of lung-cancer deaths. The risk of dying from lung cancer is 22 times higher for men who smoke and 12 times higher for women who smoke. Smoking two packs a day cuts, on average, seven years from the normal life span.

Smoking causes bronchitis, stomach ulcers, heart disease, and cancer of the lung, throat, mouth, esophagus, pancreas, and bladder. After stopping for a few years, the body clears the toxins, and the risk of these illnesses lessens considerably. Stop smoking now and you will probably add years to your life. Nearly half of all living adults who ever smoked have quit. In 1965, 40 percent of North Americans smoked cigarettes. Today that figure is below 30 percent. You or your parent can quit too.

There is much attention being paid to the fact that a number of studies have shown a drink of alcohol may be beneficial; it may even promote health. However, it should be restricted to one or two ounces of alcohol or one or two beers daily. Older adults don't tolerate excessive intake of alcohol; it can damage the brain, bone marrow, and liver. Roughly, more than three beers, three ounces of spirits, or three glasses of wine daily might be considered excessive. I have never met an elderly person who survived alcohol abuse for a prolonged period of time. Alcohol is a factor in about half of all homicides, suicides, and motor-vehicle fatalities.

Safe Driving

Motor-vehicle accidents are the fifth leading cause of death. More than half of road traffic fatalities are related to alcohol use. The good news is that older adults who don't have memory problems have fewer road traffic accidents per mile driven. They drive slower and are more cautious and defensive. However, if you are concerned about your parent's driving for any reason, such as poor eyesight, slowed reaction times, or poor judgment, it is best to first ride in the car as a passenger and observe. If you notice things that you think could lead to problems, you should discuss these with your parent. Some parents, if they are having a problem, will simply stop driving. Others become very defensive and respond, "I've been driving for fifty years or more and have never had an accident...."

If your parent will not acknowledge the problem, discuss it with your doctor. Your doctor can arrange for your parent to be retested or recommend that the license be revoked. It is my advice to you, having done this literally hundreds of times, that you let the doctor do it. Stay out of it. Parents can become very angry when they are retested and fail. They can find another doctor, but they can't find another child. Let the doctor be the bad guy.

Maintaining a Positive Mental Attitude

In the retirement home, I visited Stella, who had many aches and pains. Although she was only 60, she was riddled with anxiety and dragged down by depression. I could still be there listening to her complaints.

While I was listening to Stella, a nurse asked me to see their oldest resident, who had a mild cough. Marlene was 108. I won't soon forget her—she was independent, witty, and at peace. She complimented the nurses and loved the food. She thought the place was great. She told me about a boiled egg she'd had for breakfast—not too hard, not too soft, just perfect. She described it with reverence. She appreciated everything people did for her, like the woolen cardigan her daughter had knitted for her. Marlene was happy to receive the simple necessities of life. She was a contented person who had lived a long and enjoyable life.

How you feel has little to do with how many years you have lived. Age can bring wisdom, awareness, and a feeling of accomplishment, but if you believe that old age is a time of frailty and despair, it probably will be exactly that for you. Instead, you should feel privileged to be alive, delighted to have made it this far, and prepared to enjoy and make the best of the future.

Develop a positive self-image now. It's important to feel confident in yourself. We must accept that we can lose everything—reputation from a whisper, fortune from the stroke of a pen, family from a single accident, and health from a creature so small that a microscope can't see it. In spite of everything that can go wrong, it's important to believe in yourself so that when bad things do happen, you can survive and be happy again. Confidence and self-esteem carry us a long way.

Stay connected to the child in you who thought the world was such a wondrous place, and to the teenager who wanted to change the world and fell in love for the first time. Each of them is still inside. Life continues to provide potential for new happiness, love, fulfillment, knowledge, and wonder. To feel good about yourself, tune in and listen to yourself, your own emotions and inner signals. Tune out the world and tune into yourself. Be aware and monitor your thoughts as they bubble up spontaneously. Describe them and give them names. It will give you a clearer awareness of how you are feeling. Learn to understand yourself, think for yourself, and believe in yourself. Let the external world fade and diminish in importance. Analyze why you do things. Most of us react emotionally and then rationalize later why we felt and acted the way we did.

Don't let others choose your goals. It's important to choose your own path. You will truly know who you are and what you want when you stop struggling to please everybody else. You can finally grow and learn to accept and please yourself. By staying mentally healthy you not only help yourself, but are also able to help your parents.

Helping Your Parents Stay Positive and Optimistic

You can help your parents keep a positive mental attitude, continue to grow and seek new experiences, and enjoy themselves. Encourage them to remain open and take a few risks now and then—obviously not those that would damage health or endanger life. Parents become old when they think they are old—when they think they have seen and done it all. They need to love and be loved, continue to make new friends, and engage in social activities. I frequently see old people who have isolated themselves, because they believe "all my friends are dead or gone." There are potential friends everywhere—in the family and at neighborhood seniors centers, clubs, or church. "Act young, feel young, and you will stay young" is a proven recipe for successful aging.

Another proven recipe is an active mind. We need to keep thinking about and marveling at life and be grateful for its changes and challenges. Life will continually surprise us, so we can never afford to become complacent. How boring it would be if we knew all the answers or could decide what the next challenge was.

Most people who live into old age have strong spiritual beliefs. More than half of these people hand their problems to a higher power and rely on that power to guide them. Their faith acts as a protective mechanism to relieve anxiety and suffering. We need to understand that we don't have all the answers. Some problems are insoluble. We need to accept what we can't change and try to change what we can. The unhappy person keeps craving what he doesn't have and can't attain. The enlightened person says, "Well, this is not what I wanted, or what I asked for, but it will do. I will make the best of it."

Meditation and Prayer

Each one of us has an inner monologue, a narrative that responds to and describes how we feel at any given moment. It is confused and rambling, moving here and there in response to our environment. Beneath the constant narrative, there is a quiet spot, a refuge where we have a sense of belonging or unity with everything around us. This inner peace is our natural state, but it is often masked by the constant monologue that occurs on the surface of our minds. By becoming aware of this mindfulness, we can develop it further. Although we cannot necessarily make these periods last longer, by paying attention to them we can make them more frequent and more meaningful.

Workaholics and addicts shut the world out either by working continually or getting high. They live outside the self. Problems are temporarily forgotten. But these "solutions" actually worsen the situation that is driving the individual to negate his or her true feelings in the first place. These people become dependent on drugs or work to "forget" other problems or alleviate suffering. Mindfulness, on the other hand, is separate from action. It's a centered, peaceful, still experience.

There is growing medical research evidence to show that meditation, praying, or repeating a mantra triggers physiologic changes, lowering the breathing rate and brain-wave activity. This "relaxation response" may help healing. Prayer and meditation are effective techniques to relieve stress, as well as simple, cost-free ways to improve health and well-being.

Recently, Dr. Henry Koenig of Duke University studied 4,000 elders and found that those who went to church had better physical and mental health than those who prayed at home or had no religious activity. The rituals and practice of religion may have a calming, supportive effect. Dr. Koenig concluded that "stress and despair arise from the feeling that you are alone and there's nothing you can do about the situation. People who believe in God feel there's someone looking out for them."

More and more, doctors who have examined the effects of praying, repeating a mantra, chanting, or meditation are beginning to consider prayer and meditation as part of their approach to healing. People who pray or meditate have almost a third fewer visits to medical clinics. Prayer is not about asking or giving; it's about entering the presence of God. It works for the one who prays by acting as a trigger or release, allowing the person to hand over his or her problems and achieve a sense of relaxation.

The beauty of meditation is that you can do it anywhere. The key to this relaxation technique is breathing. This is the first and most basic exercise to center yourself. Slow your breathing by letting your breath out slowly through your mouth and take it in through your nose. Get comfortable, breathe slowly and deeply down in your abdomen, and you will automatically start to relax.

You can meditate by just breathing slowly or saying a mantra like "OOOM" or "EEEAAA," or any sound you like. Make the sound slowly and quietly. Let it take over. Concentrate on your body and relax each part of it a bit at a time. First move your toes, and then relax. Slowly move up through your body to your ankles, knees, hips, hands, moving them a little and then relaxing, until your whole body is at rest.

Now imagine some beautiful serene scene. Find a memory, a place, or an image in your mind where you can feel most at peace with yourself. It could be a desert island, a meadow, a mountain, a beach where you listen to the waves, a place where you sit watching the heavens as the world goes by. In this place in your mind, there are no troubling thoughts or feelings, just white light and peace. Another meditation technique is to close your eyes and focus your mind on the area between your two eyes or on the base of your nose. Focus your mind on this spot, then breathe deeply and relax.

Finally, look inside your mind and you will see a light. Go toward it and bathe in this white, silver, or gold light. Feel the warm light streaming through your body. Feel it healing your aches, pains, and anxiety. Come back slowly and you will be amazed at how fresh everything looks and feels. Hold onto that feeling. You can come back to it again and again.

You can go to this quiet spot when the world seems overwhelming. It's a wonderful way to relieve stress and anxiety. You might want to consider practicing meditation with your parent.

Peak Moments

During the day, there are a few precious moments when we seem to "surface" from our inner dialogue. At those times the world stands still and we are just there, living. These moments of "peak experiences" or "surfacing" offer an opportunity to review what we have been doing for the past few hours, and redirect. These are precious moments. We should never waste them but try to make the most of them and connect them together.

Try to focus on the present and attend to one thing at a time. Take time to smell, see, touch, and feel the world. This is particularly important for the sandwich generation, who often feel overwhelmed with the tasks of caring for their children and parents. It's wise to set goals and change them as soon as they have been achieved or if it's apparent you can't achieve them. Set short-term goals each day, so each day presents a challenge and has meaning. Be sure to set yourself up to succeed, not to fail.

You can control the stress in your life that is caused by uncertainty and change by keeping a grasp of the big picture. Ask yourself "What problems will I have when I am dead?" Try to accept what you can't change. You can't solve all the problems in the world; they're not your fault, and they will be here long after you are gone.

Successful people tend to rise early in the morning and have a regular rhythm to their lives. Don't lie awake at three in the morning worrying; get up early and deal with your problems. Be careful of negative emotions, too. Anger and resentment become patterns of behavior that are hard to relinquish. They are learned behaviors as addictive as drugs, gambling, or overeating. Let them go, because they are extremely damaging to health.

Fear and anxiety dull and destroy life. I see many elderly parents and family members who are full of anger, depression, and resentment. They show it in their faces, posture, and language. People who are hostile are five times more likely to develop cardiac illnesses. Practice forgiveness and understanding. Try not to judge, but learn to accept.

Laughter is a powerful, positive life force. People who laugh fare much better. Even those suffering from cancer feel better when they get together to tell jokes and laugh. They may even heal better. The power of music as a healing agent is also being recognized.

A Russian researcher who worked with very elderly Abkhazian people in the Caucasus observed that people who live longer are very loving and generous. He had never heard them use a harsh word. We can only be like this when we accept life, the world, and others, and don't try to change them. We have to learn to accept others for what they are and to share our feelings with them honestly. This brings us closer together and removes artificial barriers.

Continuing to Work

The obituaries are full of stories about people who "retired" and dropped dead a few months later. There is a difference between labor and work. Labor is an activity; work involves the mind and the body. Retirement doesn't mean your parents should stop working. Retirement offers the opportunity to work at something different. The amount of satisfaction your parents get from their work affects their health and how long they will live. We all need to work, to contribute and feel useful, to use our talents in a meaningful way.

I have a friend, a psychiatrist, who has made a study of happiness and work. He has focused on a barman at O'Hare Airport in Chicago. Every time he passes through O'Hare, my friend deliberately delays his connecting flight so he can spend a few hours with his friend, who he claims is the "consummate bartender." He can mix any cocktail known to man. He is not loud, pushy, or especially noticeable. If a customer wants to deliver a monologue, the barman will listen to all of his problems, and even provide helpful advice. If the customer wants a dialogue, the barman will join in and engage in witty and intelligent discourse. He cleans the bar, but not in a fussy, compulsive manner. He doesn't intrude or hurry. He is just there observing and serving his customers' needs. My friend thinks the barman is the most skilled artisan he has ever met. The barman loves his job. He is happy and doesn't want to do anything else. We have all met people like this. They are the glue that holds the world together.

I know doctors who make more money than 95 percent of their fellow health-care workers, yet they constantly complain that they are on call too much, don't earn enough, and want more. They are never happy with their work, family lives, or friends. Discontent robs them of enjoyment, pleasure, and satisfaction. Each of us is given a role; the greatest are not those who play the greatest roles but those who play their roles best.

Busyness is an important part of our lives and, although there comes a time in our process of aging when our energies are in decline, no one capable of work should fail to do something of value. Perhaps the greatest difficulty facing retired people is the boredom of inactivity—the lack of challenge, the blight of lack of responsibility. Any of us can volunteer to do one or many of the myriad things we learned to do in our lifetime—and perhaps the simpler the better.

Another challenge faced by adult retirees is overcoming the fear of new experiences. Retirement provides a slower lifestyle with the added benefit of surplus time. This is an excellent opportunity for the elderly to develop new skills which could benefit the community, friends, and family members.

Many retirees find personal gratification in pursuing academic excellence, discovering new interests and hobbies, and traveling, when finances permit. These combined opportunities provide the elderly with a continuum of experiences essential in maintaining self-worth.

Visiting the Doctor

I have two types of patients. One type comes, describes their problems, and hopes that I will have a pill to cure them. If I cannot deliver, they become angry or go to a different doctor. They are in denial, or angry or depressed about their illness.

The other type accepts their problems and comes to me for help. They treat me with respect and are grateful for any advice or help I have to give. They learn about their illnesses, take responsibility, and don't blame me if I can't "cure" them. These people always do better. They have come to terms with their illness, and we work together as a team to maximize their quality of life.

Smart patients

- take responsibility for their own health care;
- know what their problems are;
- know the names of the medicines they take;
- know how the medicines act and the common side effects;
- know if the medicine is working;
- know how often checkups are needed;
- know why these checkups are necessary;
- know how long they will have to take the medicine;
- know which foods and medicines (particularly over-the-counter medications) are best avoided.

Smart patients come prepared when they visit the doctor:

- They bring their medication to each visit.
- They know the purpose of each visit.
- They bring their diary and tell the doctor how they have been since the last visit.
- They come prepared with their questions; for example, What was the result of the test? Can we try a new medication? The other one made me feel too sick.

As we age, we are more likely to develop a variety of problems that can cause illness and disability. Even older adults who seem healthy should probably have a regular check-up with a doctor and a dentist to receive vaccinations and blood-pressure checks and to attend to problems before they become too serious. It is a good idea for adult children to attend these visits. When parents are failing, children should try to develop a relationship with their parents' doctors to discuss any issues they may have concerning their parents.

Choosing a Family Doctor

If a parent has moved or needs to change his or her family doctor for any reason, call the local medical society to obtain the names of doctors taking on new patients. Ask around the community about them. Most doctors are caring, diligent, attentive, and compassionate. However, some do better with older adults than others—elderly people need time more than anything else. Some physicians work more quickly than others, their waiting rooms are packed and they move patients through quickly. They rush their patients, interrupt them, and seem to order tests and prescribe a pill for every complaint. Some doctors may even damage patients' health by overtesting and overprescribing. Avoid these doctors at all costs.

A family doctor who provides good care to elders should

- "speak their language";
- take time to listen and allow time for questions and answers;
- take time to explain what the problem is and why tests or treatments are needed;
- offer choices and not dictate;
- visit at home;
- provide access to medical records and files;
- respect his or her patients and their families;
- have flexible office hours and squeeze in those who need help urgently;

- review all medications before prescribing a new one;
- have other doctors to see patients during his or her absence and arrange for these other doctors to have access to patients' files;
- answer phone calls;
- not keep scheduling return visits if they are unnecessary;
- seem interested in your parent as a person;
- give advice not only about drug treatment, but also about exercise, diet, and other preventive measures;
- take the time to write down advice and directions for medications;
- refer to specialists or get a second opinion if requested.

When it comes to your parents' health, don't take chances and don't settle for second-rate service. Get the best. If you are unhappy with a doctor, explain why and give the doctor a chance to respond and change. It's important to be able to speak your mind with your doctor. If he or she doesn't listen and improve, change doctors.

You should also change doctors if

- the waiting room is always full;
- you feel like your parents are rushed all the time;
- the doctor never seems to have time to listen;
- the doctor prescribes a new test and a new medication for each symptom;
- the doctor never checks what medications are being taken before prescribing a new one;
- each new problem requires a new visit because each visit lasts only a few minutes;
- the doctor does not seem interested in your parent as a person.

Knowing Your Medications

Whether having a test, taking a new medication, or being scheduled for surgery, patients need to know certain facts before they can give consent. They need to be informed. The health professional educates the patient, but the patient decides. An informed patient knows the range of choices available and appreciates the likely consequences of each choice.

Older patients, their family, and caregivers need to be aware of not only potential benefits, but also the possible side effects of tests and treatments. All medications are more likely to have side effects in older adults. Drugs should be given in lower doses and the doses raised slowly. In addition, older adults who take more than one medication have a greater chance of suffering side effects. Treatment given for one problem can have side effects that make other problems worse.

Older patients and caregivers need to be aware of these possibilities. They need to observe and report the effects of each new medication. They should

- know what each medication is for;
- know how each drug works in their body;
- know the effects it is likely to have on their disease;
- be aware of the common side effects;
- keep a diary and write down changes in symptoms and problems;
- know if the treatment will "cure" (curative) or control symptoms (palliative);
- carry a printout of drugs taken, allergies, and results of recent or important tests.

Although prevention is the best medicine, we often need timely investigation and treatment of problems when they occur. Many older adults need to take medicines for more than one condition such as heart disease, high blood pressure, diabetes, arthritis, and other problems. Special diets, exercise, and lifestyle changes may delay the progression of these diseases; improve quality of life; and relieve symptoms. There is no "cure" for aging or many of the diseases of aging, but proper assessment and careful treatment frequently make a huge difference.

5
Helping Parents Stay at Home

Home sweet home is where most people want to live and where most elders are happiest. Although there is a wide range of community-care choices for those who need help, the majority of care in the home is provided by family, neighbors, and friends. It is usually less expensive to provide care in the home than in institutions. For severely disabled people, institutions may be the most suitable place if family and friends do not have the expertise or resources to keep the person at home.

Older adults may have the same problem, yet require completely different solutions, depending on the setting, support systems, and mental and functional states. The care plan must be individualized and tailored to each person's needs. Wherever possible, the person must be consulted and involved in the identification of the problems and in the development and implementation of the solutions.

About 20 percent of people 65 and over who live at home need help. This can range from total care in the event of severe disability to help with a single activity such as cooking or shopping. Ninety percent of people aged 85 or more need help to stay in their homes. Most elders receive about 80 percent of their care from family or friends. Professional home-care services provide only 5 to 20 percent of care given in the home. Women provide 75 percent of the informal care, and they themselves are usually elderly and living with the person needing the care.

The goal of a home-management plan is to maintain the person safely at home while improving his or her sense of well-being. The caregiver's health should also be factored in. He or she may become burned out because the amount of care required is too much and the caregiver can't cope any longer. To care properly, it is necessary to identify and manage the medical, functional, social, emotional, environmental, and behavioral problems and to deal with them in an effective and caring fashion. There are many health and social services available in the community to help.

Elderly Denial

One of the most difficult problems I encounter in my work is the elder who lives in an unsafe environment but refuses to acknowledge this fact or make the necessary changes. Older people may feel that help or changes only serve to highlight their problems. It is very important to be sensitive to their feelings. Compromises, patience, and perseverance are often required. It is important to build trust in the relationship before any changes can be suggested or implemented. In many cases asking a doctor, pastor, trusted friend, or another person whom the elder respects to make these recommendations may be the most effective strategy in getting them to comply. Family members, particularly children, may find it frustrating that their recommendations are ignored while anything the doctor or pastor says is accepted; but this is very often the case. You should use these people to bring about the necessary changes.

Preventing Accidents

The home can be a dangerous place. After the highway, it is the location of the greatest number of fatal accidents. Older adults, who comprise 12 to 15 percent of the population, account for about 30 percent of all fatal accidents and 25 percent of all accidents. A house can tell you a great deal about the people who live there. The elderly

- like little scatter rugs they can trip on;
- wear knitted or loose-fitting slippers that offer no grip on shiny surfaces;
- often have dark, gloomy homes because of lack of paint or light bulbs that don't work;
- have stairs in poor repair;
- have cracked tiles on floors;
- often don't have smoke or fire detectors or fire extinguishers;
- have old locks, making security a problem;
- have toilet seats that are too low, loose bathroom sinks on the wall, cramped bathrooms, narrow doors into rooms, sunken baths, no shower stalls, and floors that become very slippery when wet;
- often have old stoves;
- own couches and chairs that are soft and low, making them almost impossible to get out of;
- often have broken furniture;
- have many possessions with sentimental value; these can clutter the house, make moving about hazardous, and create fire hazards.

Most elders want to continue being active. They like working outside in the garden and insist on driving. They think that since they have been managing alone for fifty years, there is no need to change now. Restricting certain activities for safety reasons while maintaining healthy mobility can be a difficult balance to achieve.

Falls are a major problem. Accidents are the fifth leading cause of death in the elderly; 75 percent of deaths from falls occur in 12 percent of the population, aged 65 or more. In community surveys of the elderly, it is estimated that the annual rate of falls is between 0.2 and 0.8 per person. About 10 percent sustain a significant injury, require hospitalization, or suffer a fracture. Of those elderly admitted to hospital as a result of a fall, only about 50 percent are alive after one year. Hip fractures, in particular, are epidemic in the elderly. In the United States, if a person lives to age 90, the chances of having a hip fracture are 32 percent for women and 17 percent for men. For all of these reasons, the first priority in any home-care plan should be safety.

As well as addressing safety concerns, changes can be made to the home to ensure that the older person can function independently for as long as possible. Most elderly people want to stay at home. It is a symbol of security, control, and autonomy. Many will leave their homes only when all else has failed. Failing health calls for an assessment, which may include discussing the need for increased services in the home, home modifications, hospitalization, treatment of medical problems, or institutionalization.

Seniors often don't want to admit they are not functioning well because they know it could be the beginning of the end. They fear that if they admit they have problems, it will be used against them to justify institutionalization. Their home, that last bastion of freedom, will be invaded by strangers. The elderly often think that having help will mean that someone will be there all the time and take over the running of the house. It is important to clarify how often the help will be there and what specific tasks they will do. Help is there to "make things easier" so the parent has more time to do other tasks or the things they enjoy.

Since many elders lack insight into their problems, it is often difficult to convince them that some modifications to the home are necessary, until they fall or have another accident. Whether or not they accept that change is necessary, it is important to remember that it is their home and that all others are only guests. Family members or professionals must never cross that line; they need to ask for permission and avoid any semblance of criticism or condemnation. It is essential to adopt a positive attitude, taking care not to embarrass the older person.

The first step in setting up a home-care plan is to do an informal assessment of your parent's home. It is impossible to do a proper home assessment without the elder present. The most valuable information is gathered by watching how the older person gets about and what tricks he uses in the home. Many elders function quite well despite an unsafe environment, while others have very dangerous habits such as standing on a broken stool in the kitchen to reach the high shelves or walking down steep, poorly lit stairs to the basement or outside on slippery or loose porch steps.

It is also essential to consider your parent's budget before making any recommendations about renovations and repairs.

Unless your parent actually agrees that there is a problem, it will be impossible to get her consent to make changes. It is not acceptable to force solutions. A skillful helper will introduce the problem so that the elder will appreciate the issues and accept the need for changes. The parent will start to see the problems as her problems, not those of a "meddling daughter" who is trying to take over. Often the key to the solution lies in the way the subject is introduced and by whom. Remember that if your parent is unwilling to accept your advice or to allow you to make modifications, then it may be advisable to involve the family doctor or another person whom your parent trusts. Get a professional to confirm your findings and to try to obtain your parent's agreement with the changes.

When you are concerned about your parent's safety, or just want to make the home as safe and functional as possible, consider the following.

Safety Check

First make sure the home has properly placed smoke alarms with live batteries. Check or install smoke detectors on all floors, including the basement. They should not be placed more than a foot below the ceiling. Because smoke rises, the higher they are, the faster they will be triggered. Insert new batteries when the time changes in the spring and fall. A carbon-monoxide detector near the bedroom should also be installed.

Ensure your parent has an escape route and a way of summoning help in an emergency. Most fire departments will do a free safety check and make suggestions. Put emergency numbers in bold letters on the phone, and make sure the phone is within easy reach. There are a wide variety of personal emergency-alert systems available that can be carried on the person to summon help in the event of a fall. Usually the device is worn around the neck or pinned to clothing. In an emergency, the wearer pushes the button on the device and a signal goes to their own telephone, which automatically dials an emergency operator. The emergency operator will then answer the call. If voice contact is not made with the emergency operator, the operator sends assistance to the home. As well, seniors centers and other agencies offer services where seniors are called regularly to check on them.

Make sure the hot-water-heater temperature is less than 110° F. Check smoking habits and use deep ashtrays around the house so that, if a cigarette is left and forgotten, it will burn out safely in the ashtray rather than fall out onto the floor. Use screens around wood stoves or space heaters, and in front of fireplaces.

Moving About

Ensure that your parent wears safe footwear. Make sure slippers fit properly and have crepe soles if possible. Good walking shoes with low heels, and ties or velcro closures, are recommended.

Check for loose mats or throw rugs on the floor. They are one of the most common hazards that lead to falls. Remove throw rugs, secure loose carpeting, and use nonskid wax on floors. I have a friend, a geriatrician, who carries a hammer and nails in his bag to nail down loose rugs and carpet. Short of removing the rugs, it is possible to put a nonslip vinyl or rubber pad under the rug, and secure the rug to the floor with double-sided tape.

Watch for small steps or thresholds that your parent may trip over. You may want to consider removing thresholds from doors or painting them a contrasting color. Adjust lighting to remove glare, and light hallways to the bedroom and bathroom. Install night lights; some are activated by loss of daylight.

Does your parent walk down to the basement on very steep, unsafe steps? Can appliances such as washer and dryer or freezer be brought upstairs to decrease the need to access the basement? Is there clutter? How can the furniture be rearranged to provide more space to get around? Is the bathroom upstairs? Can you get a commode downstairs for use during the day? Can you move the bedroom to the main level, closer to the bathroom?

Entrances and Exits

Does your parent enter the home from the road, in an elevator, or up steps? What effects do the seasons have? In winter, is the walkway icy or slippery? Where is the letter box, bus stop, and roadway? Are there any hazards, such as broken steps, cracked tiles, uneven doorways, or mats that slip underfoot? Do steps have handrails on both sides?

Is the entrance to the home wheelchair-accessible? Can friends come to visit? Does your parent hear the bell or knocker? Can you get a light to supplement the bell to indicate that someone is at the door? Remove clutter from walkways and keep paths snow and ice free. Check pathways for loose gravel, uneven surfaces, and sprung tiles or flagstones, and install handrails or lights where necessary.

Stairs

Falls on stairs usually result in serious injury. Handrails should be considered and, if installed, they must be on both sides, run the full length of the stairs, and go beyond the last step since that is the step most often missed. Make the handrail stand out by painting it a different color from the wall. It may help to have knobs or other objects marking the ends of the rail.

The edges of the stairs at the top and bottom can be painted in contrasting colors. Carpet on the stairs should be removed if it is loose, frayed, or torn. Gates can be installed at the top or bottom to prevent parents with judgment problems from falling down the stairs. It is also important to ensure that stairs are well lit.

Lighting

Light switches should be accessible so it is not necessary to grope around and over furniture to reach them. "Glow in the dark" light switches are a good idea, as are light-sensitive safety lights to provide illumination at night, particularly in bathrooms. Remember that the elderly often have cataracts, which prevents them from seeing well, even in daylight. Make sure that living areas are well lit, and bulbs have enough wattage. Just replacing 60-watt with 100-watt bulbs can make a big difference. As a general rule, there should be one 100-watt light every eight feet. Light-colored walls reflect light better, and glare can be reduced by using shades or frosted bulbs. Seek even illumination in a room by avoiding the pooling of lights.

Furniture

It is important to watch how your parent uses the furniture, how he or she walks around it, leans on it, sits on it, and gets up from it. Is it secure? Are the legs even? Does it tip when your parent gets out of it? Is it necessary to drag it around when he or she wants to use it? Does your parent stand on chairs to reach objects or crouch dangerously low to get to awkward places?

Remove caster wheels on furniture, and add rubber tips to chair legs to prevent them from slipping or skidding on the floor. Simplify the layout by removing obstacles and stumbling-blocks. Ideally the furniture should be a different color from the floor so it stands out. It may be useful to elevate the chairs and the bed so that your parent can sit with his or her legs at a ninety-degree angle, feet touching the ground. This makes it easier to get into and out of a sitting position. Putting a piece of flat plywood under cushions can make the seat firm and prevent sagging.

Electrical Wiring

Since many elders live in old homes, power switches and outlets may be loose, overloaded, or inaccessible. Placing power bars and switches closer to lights or appliances may improve access and safety. Replace all frayed cords and overloaded outlets. Make sure the power supply and wiring are up to code.

Bathroom

Most falls and injuries occur during the process of getting into and out of the tub. Rubber bath mats and textured strips in the bath provide traction and prevent falls. All bathroom mats and rugs should have a nonskid undersurface. A shower chair with a back and nonskid tips on the feet and a hand-held shower hose may reduce falls. A portable bench in the shower also makes it possible to shower while sitting. Install grab bars in the shower and tub. Water-temperature regulation will prevent scalds. Consider changing faucets to the lever type that can be manipulated more easily than regular faucets, or install adapters to existing fixtures to allow for better control.

Make sure the toilet is easily accessible. Older adults often experience an urgent need to pass urine and must get to the toilet quickly. If the bathroom is on the second floor, it may be useful to have a commode or urinal on the main floor. Many toilet seats are too low for the elderly; there are a wide variety of toilet-seat lifts available. A bar to provide a solid support when rising from the toilet can make all the difference, but it must be installed in the appropriate place and at the right height. Grab bars are often installed at a thirty-degree angle.

Bedroom

Many older adults spend more than ten hours a day in bed, making the bedroom the most used room in the house or apartment. It is important to make movement to and from the bed as safe as possible. Check the height of the bed and the firmness of the mattress. The bed should be at least three or four feet from the wall. Your parent should be able to sit on the bed with his or her knees bent at ninety degrees and feet just touching the floor. Bed rails should be used only if your parent has been rolling out of bed.

Consider the need for a bedside commode at night. Make sure the hallway to the bathroom is well lit and obstacle free. Smoking in bed should be strictly forbidden. Ensure that the telephone, light switches, and bedside table are within easy reach so your parent does not have to stretch too far and risk falling out of bed.

Lower the closet clothes bar and install hooks to keep contents more accessible.

Kitchen

Relocating objects to more accessible places can increase safety and independence. In the kitchen, ensure easy access to commonly used dishes and utensils. Avoid shelves beyond safe and easy reach. Kitchen footstools should have handrails and rubber tips on the feet.

Watch your parent preparing meals and cooking. Is the routine safe? Make sure he or she does not wear clothing with loose ends or hanging sleeves when cooking. If your parent is using unsafe cooking techniques, or forgetting to use the right burner, it may be necessary to disconnect and cover all but one burner. Make sure stove dials are clearly marked for low, med, high, and off positions. One burner with one knob is less confusing. Try to introduce a microwave; it's safer when used properly. You could also consider installing a master switch for the oven so it can be disconnected when you or another caregiver is not around. A Meals-on-Wheels or homemaker service is another option.

Use lightweight small appliances. Handles on pots should be heat-resistant, and elders should be encouraged to use carts or boards to carry hot dishes rather than carrying them themselves. A heat-proof counter or counter mat next to the stove makes it possible to slide rather than lift pots off the stove for those with a weak grip. Finally, get a whistling kettle with an automatic switch that turns the appliance off when the water boils.

Assistive Devices

It is not uncommon to see an older person using an assistive device such as a walker, wheelchair, or even a walking stick in an unsafe manner. These devices are very helpful if they are used correctly, but can actually increase the risk of falls if used incorrectly. It is important to have a professional pick out the most appropriate device and teach the person how to use it. It is also essential to make sure that any device used is in good repair. If your parent has specific foot problems, he or she should see a podiatrist for treatment.

Safeguarding the Home for Alzheimer's Patients

There are many useful ways to adapt a home for an individual with Alzheimer's, and a variety of other strategies to deal with the myriad problems the Alzheimer's patient presents. A suitable environment makes living safer, increases the person's independence, and allows the caregiver to relax knowing the person is safe.

Too many changes may upset your parent, so it's important not to make changes for the sake of them. Some of the following changes can be expensive, but others are cheap. They can pay for themselves over and over again.

Wandering

Alzheimer's patients are usually active, even late in the illness, so they tend to wander. Without regular activity, they become anxious and agitated. They should be allowed to wander in the greatest area possible. Fence in the backyard or put ropes or gates across open sidewalks and driveways if the area is already fenced, and let them wander in and out of the house as they wish. They should exercise every day.

Take them to the park in summer and for walks in the shopping mall during colder weather.

If you are the primary caregiver, ask your neighbours to phone you if they see your parent on the street without you. They may even walk with your parent and steer him or her back home. Make sure the phone number and address are stitched into your parent's clothes. You should also consider putting your parent's name on the Wandering Patient Registry. Your local police take his or her name and photo. They are trained to deal with wandering Alzheimer's patients, and if wandering occurs, a photo is more helpful than an instruction to look for a "small, gray-haired man with glasses."

Obviously one does not want to build a prison or a death trap in a fire, but there are some simple ideas that should be considered. Put locks on the doors at the top or bottom out of the normal line of vision. If you have to, cover the door with a curtain. Put double locks or dead bolts on the main exit doors.

Falls

This subject has been covered elsewhere in the book, but there are a few extra precautions for Alzheimer's patients. They fall because of poor judgment and also because they lose depth perception as well as experiencing the normal vision problems associated with aging. Get rid of swinging chairs and rocking chairs. Keep rooms clutter-free. Round off the corners of furniture with covers or tape.

Tips

- Lock pills away. Keep shampoo, cosmetics, and other items that could be swallowed out of reach.
- You may have to cover mirrors. Patients may not recognize themselves in the mirror and think there's a stranger in the house.

- Put some colored tape around the edge of the bathtub or toilet to make it stand out.
- Use nonskid flooring with sharp contrasts between the fixtures and the floor.
- Put light-activated night lights in the hallways, bedroom, and bathroom.
- Take the lock off the bathroom door as patients will lock themselves in.
- Make sure the wastepaper basket is not next to the toilet or shaped like the toilet or it will be used as one.
- You may want to ration toilet paper; people with Alzheimer's sometimes use too much and clog the toilet.
- Install a lock on the thermostat.
- Put the sharp knives and dangerous appliances away.
- Take the dials or knobs off the stove when it's not in use, or cover the elements, or put a master switch on the stove. Take out the fuses if necessary. Alternatively, get a master switch for the gas, or switch off the circuit breaker for the stove.
- Keep the kitchen bare and simple. Serve lots of finger foods and snacks in addition to regular small meals. Leave snacks out all the time. Use plastic dishes and large blunt-handled utensils. Serve food cut up.
- Put plastic safety latches on the cupboards you want to keep your parent away from. Put plastic plugs in the electric outlets. Hide sink stoppers to avoid overflow.
- In the later stages, you may need a gate at the top, or bottom, of the stairs.
- If your parent smokes, put deep ashtrays throughout the house.
- Use motion-activated lights outside at night. If the patient does go outside, the lights going on may wake you. Or put buzzers on the exit doors.
- Give away or throw out poisonous plants.
- Block off hot radiators or cover them to prevent scalds.
- You may have to close off the fireplace and swimming pool.

- Mark sliding glass doors with decals to stop your parent from walking into them.
- Get an exercise machine, either a stationary bike or a walking machine.
- In an apartment building, mark the floor on the elevator's controls and mark the apartment door so they will recognize it. Mark the bedroom door and bathroom door to prompt them.
- When your parent is agitated, don't turn on the television. Try to play soothing music instead.

Getting Help

Contact the Alzheimer's Association and get all the help you can (see page 32). You can't do it alone and you need to realize this as soon as possible. Caring for an Alzheimer's patient is grueling, and you need to take time out to sit on the bench like a hockey player and catch your breath. If you try to do it alone, you will become exhausted. A burned-out caregiver is no good to anyone.

Even though you may not want to, join a support group. Educate yourself and, most of all, go easy on yourself.

6

Planning Alternative Living Arrangements

A growing number of specialized living arrangements and community-based health- and personal-care services are now available for older adults. For many, these community services and alternative living arrangements offer an option to nursing-home care and allow them to remain in the community. For others, however, there is no substitute for a good nursing home.

Long-Term Care

My mother made me promise never to put her in a nursing home. She became more forgetful after my father died. She started burning pots and pans, stopped paying her bills, lost weight, and refused help. One day she had a small fire in the kitchen and the fire department was called. She had burned herself slightly. They took her to Emergency and she was admitted to hospital. She refused to accept any help and, although the hospital social worker didn't want to let her go home, we let her try one more time anyway. She fell and broke her hip. After that, she went to the nursing home. She never forgave me. Every time I went to visit her, she begged me to take her home and accused me of putting her in prison. It was awful. I swear I will never do this to my children. I would never put my children through it.

No matter what technological advances are made in health care, we will never stop people from getting old and dying, and there will always be a need for nursing homes. When the elderly become too confused or frail to live at home, they must move to a supervised setting, often a retirement or nursing home. Parents should not make unreasonable demands on their children by making them promise to "never put me in a nursing home." This can be a curse. At times, the needs of older relatives can become such a heavy burden that families cannot provide enough care at home and are forced to place them in a nursing home. If parents at one time insisted they didn't want this, children can be left haunted by feelings of betrayal and guilt.

Planning for shelter in old age is a crucial part of long-term planning. Although only 5 percent of those aged 65 or more live in long-term-care facilities, at least one-third of the population spend some time in them. Accurate, up-to-date information about the long-term-care system can be obtained from a variety of different sources: local community information centers, placement-coordination services, social workers in geriatric centers, family doctors, community health nurses, or local hospitals.

If you think your parent should be in a nursing home, the first step is to determine if she is still able to live in her own home. An assessment of her medical, physical, emotional, and social needs is required to determine her requirements and arrange the appropriate community services. If possible, the medical part of the assessment should be done by a doctor who specializes in the care of the elderly, such as a geriatrician. A proper assessment determines the range of problems and possible solutions. Services will be mobilized in the home, or the elder will be moved to a facility.

In general, there are four types of long-term-care facilities providing care, depending on the person's needs: retirement homes, nursing homes, homes for the aged, and chronic-care hospitals. These facilities make up the long-term-care system. Referrals to the system are made through a central agency, the placement-coordination service, which employs a standard assessment to determine the person's care needs. Based on this assessment, the person is streamed into one of four different levels. In retirement homes, residents can do their own basic care but get medications and meals. In nursing homes and homes for the aged, residents get help with some basic care. In chronic care, they have all their basic care needs provided.

One of the biggest problems in caring for the elderly is that those who need help often fail to realize it. Elderly people with hearing problems, visual deficits, and memory loss are often not aware of their problems, or deny that they have problems. They just don't realize how serious these problems are and say, "I've been living (driving, cooking, taking care of myself) alone, for fifty years, without any problems, why should I need help now?" or "I have been driving for sixty years, never had an accident; there's no problem with my driving." One of the hallmarks of serious memory loss in old age is the elderly person's lack of insight into just how threatening the problem is. These elders refuse to participate in planning solutions.

Because of this, it's important to plan in advance. If a spouse or child has been assigned power of attorney for personal care and shelter, this person is entitled to make the decision to place the elder in a nursing home if the need arises. If the ability to understand or appreciate the situation is lacking, the elder lacks the capacity (competency) to make this decision and the power of attorney can make it for him or her. However, the older person can leave strict instructions about the circumstances under which he or she will go into an institution, and which institution. For example, an elder might write: "I want to stay at home as long as possible. I never want to go in as long as there is only a reasonable health risk at home. I don't mind losing weight or falling, but don't let me burn the apartment down and put my neighbors at risk. I would prefer to live six months at home rather than three years in a home. Don't ever tie me up in restraints except for a short period of time if I need a medical treatment. A copy of an advance directive for personal care and shelter is enclosed" (see page 186).

People who accept the fact that they may have to live in an institution fare much better when they have to go. Those who try everything to avoid going to one often fail to come to terms with it when it happens. When it is time to consider institutions, it's important to obtain the right information in order to make the best decision. Many people must spend the last years of their life in institutions; the choice of home can seriously affect their quality of life. Better to acknowledge that there may be a need, and plan well ahead, than to deny it will be necessary, and leave family members scrambling to find the first available home in a crisis.

Retirement Homes/Lodging Homes

Rest and retirement homes and lodging homes are run by private groups and vary from small, supervised homes to large, luxurious buildings. Residents generally pay for meals, housekeeping, supervision, and personal care. The homes are subject to public-health standards for fire and building safety. Retirement homes range from modest establishments providing basic shelter, food, and minimal supervision to luxury retirement complexes with extensive personal services and recreational activities.

Retirement homes are ideal for those who no longer want to live alone and can perform basic activities of daily living, such as grooming, walking, dressing, and feeding, independently. They remain involved in their usual activities, keep in touch with family, and have a ready-made social network in the home. As in a hotel, meals and housekeeping are provided.

Most retirement facilities have a security and emergency service. Medications are usually dispensed, and home-care services such as physiotherapy, occupational therapy, and some nursing services may be available. Residents can purchase nursing or homemaking services if necessary. The family doctor can continue to provide care, or most facilities offer their own staff doctor if required.

Rooms may be private, semiprivate, or standard (three or more in a room), with shared or private bathrooms. If the budget allows, suites or private apartments are available. Rooms are furnished, but residents are encouraged to bring their own furniture and possessions. Meal service ranges from a single meal to three meals a day. With less than full-meal service, there are kitchen facilities in each room. Friends and family are welcome in the dining room. Room service is negotiable. Some homes include laundry service; others provide washing machines and dryers. Although most homes offer some recreational activities, the staffing, supervision, and organization differ from home to home.

Nursing Homes

Nursing homes provide care for those who require about one and a half hours to two and a half hours of nursing care and personal care every day. These needs are determined by criteria used by placement-coordination services. Some of these facilities also offer respite services (a short-term stay for a month or so).

The selection of a suitable nursing home requires research, knowledge, and planning. It's important to gather the necessary facts before choosing a facility, because there is a wide variety of homes, ranging from good to bad, to downright ugly. The place you choose may be your parent's home for the rest of his or her life. Licensing requirements have minimal acceptable standards for care and services. Government inspectors visit nursing homes regularly to ensure that they comply with these standards.

Nursing homes are owned and operated by for-profit or nonprofit corporations. Some are part of chains. Others are sponsored by religious, charitable, or municipal groups. The responsibility for the operation of the nursing home belongs to its governing body, which is legally licensed by the province to operate the facility. This governing body sets policies, makes rules, and enforces them for the residents' health and safety. An administrator runs the home on a day-to-day basis.

Each resident in a nursing home is under the care of a physician. If the person's family doctor cannot continue to provide care, a new physician takes over. Physicians determine each resident's needs and prescribe medical care, programs (including diets), physical restraints, and medications. Each resident has a complete physical examination on admission. The medical plan is based on these findings.

Government financial aid is available for those who cannot afford to pay the full cost of nursing-home care.

Chronic Care

Chronic care is provided in some acute care or chronic care/rehabilitation hospitals. To be eligible for chronic care, residents require more than two and a half hours of skilled nursing and personal care daily and must meet specific admission criteria. Chronic-care units may also offer services such as palliative care and special programs for behavior problems.

Chronic-care hospitals provide short-term rehabilitation or long-term care. When a person requires regular, frequent care by a skilled health-care professional, the most appropriate setting in which to deliver this is a chronic-care hospital. Many nursing homes and homes for the aged cannot deal with frequent dressings, tubes, catheters, certain mechanical lifts, or severely disturbed residents. Such patients often require more hands-on care than nursing homes can provide. Residents may be required to make quarterly payments, which are adjusted to reflect the amount of care required.

Some chronic-care hospitals offer respite programs, which take people in from the community for a designated period of time, usually from two to four weeks. Respite services provide relief to caregivers who provide care for the elderly in their homes or apartments within the community. The older person usually goes into the center while the caregiver takes a "vacation." There is a fee for this service, but it may be subsidized by government or community clubs. There can be a big demand for respite services, so it's important to book well ahead of time.

Choosing a Home

If long-term care for your parent may be necessary in the future, it is important to plan ahead. Good homes often have long waiting-lists, and the chance of getting the home of your choice increases if application is made in advance. Families have been known to create a crisis to jump to the top of the list, especially when a place in the desired nursing home becomes available. Discussion and planning prepares the elder for the move. If a nursing home is chosen in an emergency, it is more likely that a bad choice may be made. A suitable home can make all the difference to your parent's quality of life.

There are a number of things that can be done in advance:

- Learn about the long-term-care system, particularly the level that your parent will be using.
- Ask around; find out about the different nursing homes in your area.
- Ask friends who work in the health-care industry what the different nursing homes are like.
- Visit the ones in your area and talk to relatives or friends who might know people in these homes.
- Scan the media for nursing-home news.
- Order as many booklets and brochures as possible from the different social-service agencies.
- Get a guide to the local homes if one is available.

If you know someone in a nursing home, visit and ask him or her about it. Pay particular attention to patient care, staffing, meals, cleanliness, maintenance, and social programs. If the place smells, the staff are rude, and all the residents are slumped over, tied into their chairs, and staring glassy-eyed out the windows, it doesn't matter what the glossy brochures, administrator, or directors say—forget it. If the place is clean, the staff are friendly and courteous, the residents seem contented, and there are some activities going on, consider it. If you go to visit someone, drop in at meal time. Check out the food. Is the hot food hot and the cold food cold? Would you eat it? Are the radios in the residents' rooms playing rock-'n'-roll music, selected by the staff? Is the television channel selected by the staff so they can watch their favorite soap? Is the home set up for the staff or the residents?

Drop by again in the middle of the morning or afternoon. Are there any activities? How hard do they really try? Are the residents gathered on the third floor of an apartment-style building in a room off a long, shiny corridor? Or are they in a ground-floor room, looking out on a nice garden with a bird-feeder?

In business there are three important factors that determine success: "location, location, and location." It's much the same for nursing homes. If the home down your street is pretty crummy compared with the one ten miles and four bus changes away, it may be better to have your parent down the street because the family can visit more often and supplement the substandard services. A home nearby is more convenient for family, friends, relatives, and the family doctor. It's important to maintain as much continuity as possible in the resident's life. The move itself is disruptive enough.

Size of the home is another important consideration. Larger homes may have more activities, while smaller homes may provide more individual and personal service. What would your parent prefer? Where possible, the elder should also visit the homes to make her own choices.

You should make an appointment with the administrator and do the "official tour." Have a list of questions ready. Remember they are selling their home like any salesperson pushes a product. How rigid are the rules? One accepts that there must be some rules, but do rules come before the residents' dignity, freedom, and well-being? Are visiting hours flexible? Can you take your parent out whenever you want? Do you have to apply in advance and fill out forms for every little thing? Obtain a list of all the basic room rates, semiprivate and private rates, extra costs, and a copy of the contract. Are there any hidden costs or extra charges for professional or other services such as television or personal care? How much of your parent's furniture, pictures, and bedclothes can be used? If your parent goes to hospital, does she lose her bed? How long will they hold it?

Sing-songs and social activities can really increase the quality of life of nursing-home residents. A bar and pub night can be a wonderful evening for older people. Is it a religious home run by serious fundamentalists in gray suits who don't eat ice cream and don't allow music, laughter, or singing? Forget it. Is there easy access to television, films, or radio? Is there a small library? Do you feel "at home" there or does it feel like a bus station?

If your parent must share a room, the roommate is absolutely key to his or her quality of life. Can you have a say in roommate selection? Can your parent change roommates if it's not working out?

Observe how medications are dispensed. What is the average number of medications per resident? If the home is using more than five or six medications (including laxatives), you may want to consider another facility, because the residents are probably overmedicated.

What percentage of the residents have physical restraints? Does the home have a physical-restraint policy? If the home puts physical restraints on a resident without discussing it with the resident and the family, do not even consider the home. Too many long-term-care institutions abuse the use of physical restraints. They should, at a minimum, discuss the use of restraints with the resident, if competent, and with the family, if not. The staff should provide an opportunity for the resident and family to meet and discuss current issues on a regular basis.

Finally, it's important to ask if the nursing home provides palliative care. Will your parent be kept comfortable when he or she is dying, or just be shipped off to the nearest emergency department. Better homes provide palliative care to ensure dignity and comfort at the end of life. This is essential.

Making the Move as Easy as Possible

The move into the nursing home affects the whole family. It takes time to adjust to the new living arrangements. Some nursing homes offer preadmission conferences or family conferences for residents and family members. The family should accompany the parent on moving day and spend as much time as possible with him or her in the next days, weeks, and months to help with settling in and becoming accustomed to the new surroundings. Personal items such as furniture, quilts, pictures, or floor coverings make the new room comfortable and familiar.

Schedule family visits as regularly and as frequently as possible to avoid gaps. Family visits mean so much, as do little gifts like candies, jellies, chocolates, new photos, or mementoes to make each visit special and memorable. The morale of residents whose families visit is higher than the morale of those whose families don't. They also may receive better care from the staff because they realize the family are monitoring the care and may drop in at any time.

Tell the staff if you are satisfied with the care. Gifts at Christmas, New Year's, and Easter show how much you appreciate the staff and affect their attitude toward the resident. If the family is always complaining, the staff will develop a negative attitude. If the family is helpful, generous, and thoughtful, the staff will respond accordingly. Families who project their guilt and anger at the staff do nothing to improve the care of their parent or other residents. The staff ends up spending their time coping with dysfunctional families rather than with the residents. Try to be supportive, unless you believe your parent is actually being abused or neglected.

Simple activities like shopping, bowling, swimming, indoor golf, picture-album review, or crafts like painting, tooling, and ceramics are easy and fun to do with your parent. In summer, walking, gardening, croquet, trips to the beach, barbecues, picnics, or visits to botanical gardens are enjoyable. Don't give up. If you and other family members don't visit because "it's too difficult," go in pairs and spell each other off. Just a drive in the car can sometimes be enough. Have a picnic in your parent's room if he or she is too frail to leave. Make a note of birthdays and special anniversaries and plan to share them together.

Follow-Up in the Home

Sometimes residents show physical or mental changes after they have been admitted. This can be caused by the adjustment to the new environment or the use of certain medications. Be aware of these possible changes. The family should be able to at least access the list of medications the resident is taking and be able to discuss this issue with staff at the home.

Theft can be a problem in some nursing homes. Find out if it is safe to leave jewelry, valuables, and ornaments in the residents' rooms. Is there any grievance mechanism? A residents' council involves residents in the decision making and provides a process for dealing with any difficulties residents and families may have. Is there a residents' council? Find out if you can be a volunteer in the home and if any seniors, church groups, or schoolchildren come to help out with care or with social events.

Admission papers should include the resident's Bill of Rights and an agreement with the terms and conditions, the daily room rate, services included, and costs of extra services. Minimum services such as nursing care, meals, social activities, and personal care are covered by the basic rate. Facilities should provide an itemized bill for each requested payment. And, finally, if worst comes to worst and you feel your parent is being abused or neglected, change homes and report the facility to the authorities.

7
Legal and Financial Planning

It's becoming obvious that the state will not cover all our health-care expenses in the future. As we face the prospect of living longer, we also face the possibility of more years of disability with a limited ability to live independently. Our ability to perform activities of daily living independently (dressing, cooking, shopping, grooming) may decline, and we may need help in our own homes or need to move to a facility where we can receive adequate supervision and help. Many of these services are not covered by government-funded programs, and we may have to pay for them ourselves. Financial security may mean the difference between staying at home or going into an institution, between comfort and scrimping to get by.

Financially, there are three phases in the life cycle. The first is a period of dependency as children grow to adult life. The second phase is the "earning period" when adults work, gather capital, and save for retirement. The third is the post-retirement phase, when retirees usually live off pensions and accumulated capital.

During a lifetime, people earn a limited amount of money. They should use it wisely to ensure financial security in old age. Since many without chronic illnesses now live into their nineties, it seems reasonable to plan to live for ninety years. This is a long period post-retirement for those who retire at 65. Only about 5 per cent of the population continue to accrue money after retirement. The vast majority of retired people are concerned with maintaining their lifestyle without using up their savings.

Financial concerns are one of the greatest sources of worry throughout life. They are often unstated and may remain constant between parents and children. Children are concerned that parents will not have enough money and will need their help. Parents are worried they will run out of money and become a financial drain on their children. Older adults that do not have financial security feel trapped and don't know where or to whom to turn. Some, their savings wiped out by recessions, inflation, deflation, and changing interest rates, are forced to turn to their children.

Maintaining Assets after Retirement

There are two issues of major concern to retirees: maintaining their assets and distributing them after death. They want to maintain their lifestyle by living off the interest from their principal and their pensions without diminishing their net worth. Older adults must also decide how they will distribute their assets after death. They may consider the financial and non-financial needs of their beneficiaries to ensure fairness in the distribution of these assets. In addition, many want to ensure a smooth transferral of resources without too much shrinkage from death taxes. The goal of proper financial planning is to balance all of these goals.

The first step is to gather as much documentation and information as possible—deeds, mortgages, receipts for bonds, stocks, bank books, insurance policies, and so on. Be prepared to discuss financial issues openly so the areas that need attention can be highlighted and dealt with first. Any shortfalls will be identified at this stage. When these documents have been gathered and organized, it is important to make sure they are photocopied and that duplicates are kept for safety. If they are kept in a safety deposit box, remember to give someone else access as the box may be sealed by the bank after death or in the event of serious illness.

The papers should then be organized into a financial statement. I have provided a simple list of these documents in Table I. Tables II and III provide a sample list of assets and expenses to allow children to help parents develop a reasonable financial plan.

TABLE I—CHECKLIST
OF ORIGINAL DOCUMENTS

Parents should inform children where these documents are kept for easy retrieval if necessary.

Personal:	Yes	No	N/A
Driver's Licence	☐	☐	☐
Social Insurance No.	☐	☐	☐
Health Insurance No.	☐	☐	☐
Marriage Licence(s)	☐	☐	☐
Military Documents	☐	☐	☐
Divorce Papers	☐	☐	☐
Your Will	☐	☐	☐
Spouse's Will	☐	☐	☐
Power of Attorney	☐	☐	☐
Trusts	☐	☐	☐
Others	☐	☐	☐

_____

_____

_____

_____

Financial:	Yes	No	N/A
Bank Book(s)	☐	☐	☐
Safety Deposit Box Keys	☐	☐	☐
Combination for Safe	☐	☐	☐
Certificates of Deposit	☐	☐	☐
Checking Account(s)	☐	☐	☐
Insurance Policies	☐	☐	☐
Pension Plans	☐	☐	☐
Property Deeds	☐	☐	☐
Mortgages	☐	☐	☐
Bank Loan(s)	☐	☐	☐
Credit Card Statement(s)	☐	☐	☐
Income Tax Return(s)	☐	☐	☐
Retirement Plans/Pension	☐	☐	☐
Stock Certificates	☐	☐	☐
Trust Agreements	☐	☐	☐

TABLE II—ASSETS AND LIABILITIES

Liquid Assets
Cash (checking and savings accounts) _____
Short-Term Investments _____
Cash Value of Life Insurance _____

Total Liquid Assets: _____

Investments
Home _____
Real Estate Investments _____
Stocks _____
Bonds _____
Retirement and/or Pension Plan(s) _____

Other Investment(s)   _____

_____   _____

_____   _____

_____   _____

_____   _____

Total Investment Assets: _____

Personal Assets

Furnishings   _____

Car   _____

Artwork/Antiques   _____

Total Personal Assets: _____

TOTAL ASSETS: $_____

Short-Term Obligations

Outstanding Credit   _____

Mortgage on Personal Residence   _____

Borrowings on Life Insurance   _____

Bank Loan(s)   _____

Loan(s)   _____

Income Taxes   _____

Credit Cards   _____

Other(s)

_____   _____

_____   _____

Total Short-Term Obligations: _____

Long-Term Obligations

Loans to Purchase
  Investment Assets _____

Loans to Purchase Personal
  Assets _____

Total Long-Term Obligations: _____

TOTAL LIABILITIES: $_____

Total Assets _____
  Minus Total Liabilities _____

Equals **NET WORTH:** $_____

TABLE III—INCOME VERSUS EXPENSES

Retirement Income:	**You**	**Spouse**	**Total**
Social Security	_____	_____	_____
Company Pension	_____	_____	_____
Personal Employment	_____	_____	_____
Benefits	_____	_____	_____
Other	_____	_____	_____
Total Retirement Income:	_____	_____	_____

Investment Income	**You**	**Spouse**	**Total**
Taxable Interest	_____	_____	_____
Non-Taxable Interest	_____	_____	_____
Dividends	_____	_____	_____
Rents (net cash of expenses)	_____	_____	_____
Investment partnerships	_____	_____	_____
Social Security	_____	_____	_____

Pension Trust Fund(s) _____ _____ _____
Other _____ _____ _____
_____ _____ _____

**Total Retirement
Income** _____ _____ _____

**TOTAL INCOME FROM
INVESTMENTS:** $_____ $_____ $_____

Fixed Expenses

_____ _____
_____ _____
_____ _____
_____ _____
_____ _____
_____ _____
_____ _____
_____ _____
_____ _____
_____ _____
_____ _____
_____ _____
_____ _____
_____ _____
_____ _____
_____ _____
_____ _____
_____ _____
_____ _____
_____ _____

TOTAL FIXED EXPENSES: $_____

In going through this exercise, be patient and keep at it. Don't leave it until later; it may be too late.

Once you have pinpointed your parents' financial strengths and weaknesses, you may want some outside help from a financial consultant about any necessary changes. Many parents scrimp so their children will inherit their savings. Children may have to give parents permission to spend it on themselves. They may have to say, "Mom, all your life you have been saving for a rainy day. Well, the rainy day is here, so why don't you enjoy your savings?"

The common problem for older adults is to live comfortably without using up their principal. The challenge is to find the best way to distribute assets so that living expenses are covered and there is enough for an emergency. Some of the principal should be kept in short-term investments that can be easily accessed if necessary. It may be useful to plan in three- to five-year periods. Try, if possible, to allow for inflation.

The other problem is to balance return against risk. Older men and women have seen many ups and downs in the financial world and may not accept risk as well as their children do. They will often choose security over profit or a large return. They cannot afford to lose money because they cannot earn it back again. Rather than playing the stock market, they will often opt for lower-yield investments like government bonds. Part of their income may be placed in short-term bonds, and a portion in long-term bonds with a slightly better yield.

It is desirable to diversify investments as much as possible. Mutual funds offer diversity and professional management. Some offer easy access and can be liquidated easily. Guidance about investments and use of assets is well beyond the scope of this book. However, a reminder about taxes is in order. Death taxes can be avoided by careful financial planning. Be sure to ask your financial adviser about strategies.

Protecting Your Parents' Interests

Medical technology enables people to live longer, but often this extra time on earth is spent with some form of chronic mental and/or physical disability. Unless these eventualities have been planned for, family and friends have to make decisions for the incapacitated. They may be forced to make decisions that can haunt them for the rest of their lives. These decisions can also lead to family feuds that turn into extended wars. Before an illness strikes that will render an elder incapable of making a decision, parents should make their wishes known. This will protect the parents, their family, and their friends.

Several legal vehicles can protect parents' interests and allow them to plan ahead. These devices include powers of attorney, advance directives, guardianships, wills, and trusts. Properly used, they protect parents' interests and save families emotional and psychological trauma. Too many parents plan for death only by completing wills, forgetting that it is probably more important to plan for living with incapacity or disability. Proper planning will ensure that parents are spared government bureaucrats taking charge of their affairs.

Power of Attorney

This is a legal document that allows an individual (the person who gives this power, the principal or grantor) to hand over power to manage financial affairs to another (the attorney). It is a flexible arrangement or contract. The attorney can receive sweeping or very specific powers. For example, someone could be given power of attorney to sign a single document on a certain date. A regular power of attorney ceases once the principal becomes incapacitated for any reason. To extend the usefulness of the power of attorney, a durable or "continuing" power of attorney was developed which continues in force even in the event of incapacity.

A power of attorney document must be signed and witnessed. The witnesses cannot be marital or business partners of the principal or the attorney. The number of witnesses and who they must be depends on the province in which it is signed. Some jurisdictions require witnessing by a notary public and registration with the government.

The power-of-attorney document gives the attorney the ability to transact any business that is authorized in the document. It does not give the attorney the right to do anything that is not permitted by the principal. Nonetheless, the contract is a very strong document. It gives the attorney sweeping powers over the principal's financial affairs. For this reason, the principal should have complete confidence in the attorney. To appoint an attorney, the principal should understand:

- what assets are owned;
- what obligations are owed to dependants;
- that a specific or general power of attorney can be given;
- that the power can be revoked;
- that the attorney could misuse this power.

Legislation has been passed across the United States to broaden powers of attorney to cover not only finances, but also personal care, health care, shelter, and property. These laws allow people to plan ahead and appoint different attorneys for different areas in their lives.

If there is any question about the capacity of the principal at the time that the power of attorney is being granted, a letter from a doctor or other qualified professional should accompany it, confirming that the person was capable and understood what he was doing. A power of attorney can be given only by a competent person. Once the principal becomes incapacitated, the person who received the power of attorney acts on his or her behalf.

Advance Directives

An advance directive is any written document that express-es a person's wishes in advance. The most common form of advance directive is the *will*. A will contains specific instructions—directives—about what we want done with our possessions after our death. A slightly different kind of advance directive is a *power of attorney*, which empowers another person to act on our behalf if we become unable to make decisions ourselves.

Another kind of advance directive deals specifically with health and personal care. It contains instructions about our care in case we are not able to make health- or personal-care decisions for ourselves. For example, at some future time we could become incapacitated by illness or injury. This could affect our ability to think, reason, and speak. The "Let Me Decide" Health Care Directive (see page 186) enables us to let others know our wishes about medical treatment.

As long as we remain competent—able to consider and communicate choices—we can make decisions for our-selves. An advance directive is used only if we are unable to make our wishes known.

There are two types of advance directives: "instruction-al" and "proxy."

An *instructional directive* gives specific instructions. It states what treatments are wanted or not wanted under any given circumstance. These documents are also called "Living Wills." A statement can be as general or as specific as you want. The more specific the statements are, the eas-ier it will be for family and doctors to follow. An instruc-tional directive is not limited to treatment of terminal or irreversible conditions; it can also apply to curable, reversible conditions.

A *proxy directive* nominates another person (the proxy) to make decisions for your health and personal care if you become incompetent. These documents are also called

"Medical Powers of Attorney" or "Patient Advocate Designations." The proxy has the ability to make health- and personal-care decisions in much the same way as a power of attorney can for financial matters.

The "Let Me Decide" Health Care Directive has an instructional and a proxy directive (a Living Will and a Medical Power of Attorney/Patient Advocate Designation). This ensures that a parent's wishes are followed. If written instructions are not specific enough to guide a doctor in all situations, the proxy can provide additional information and directions.

"LET ME DECIDE"
Health- and Personal-Care Directive

1. INTRODUCTION

In this Directive I am stating my wishes for my health and personal care should the time ever come when I am not able to communicate because of illness or injury. This Directive should never be used if I am able to decide for myself. It must never be substituted for my judgment if I can make these decisions.

If the time comes when I am unable to make these decisions, I would like this Directive to be followed and respected. Please do everything necessary to keep me comfortable and free of pain. Even though I may have indicated that I do not want certain treatments, I recognize that these may be necessary to keep me comfortable. I understand that my choices may be overridden if the treatment is necessary to maintain comfort.

I have thought about and discussed my decision with my family, friends, and my family doctor. In an emergency, please contact my power(s) of attorney/substitute decision maker(s) or my family doctor listed below. If these people are not available, then please do as I have requested in this Directive.

I, _____,
revoke any previous power of attorney for personal and
health care made by me and APPOINT:

_____

*jointly and severally** to act as my power of attorney (proxy,
mandatory). If he/ she/ they is/are unable, unwilling or
predeceases me, then I appoint as alternate

_____

substitute(s), power of attorney(s) (proxies, mandatories)
to act *jointly and severally** as my substitute(s) or attorney(s)
for personal care.

Dated and signed this

_____ day of _____ 19_____.

_____
Signature

_____
Print Name

_____
Health Card No.

*If you've named more than one substitute (attorney, proxy, or mandato-
ry) or more than one alternate and you want each of them to have
the authority to act separately, leave the words "jointly or severally." If you want them to act together, not independently, delete
"and severally" and leave "jointly." If you have named one person, delete "jointly and severally."

2. PERSONAL STATEMENT

I would consider an irreversible condition to be any condition

_____

_____

_____

_____

_____

_____

_____

_____

_____

_____

_____

_____

_____

_____

_____

I would agree to the following procedures: (write YES or NO)

Blood Transfusion   _____

Organ Donation   _____

Post Mortem   _____

Cremation   _____

3. THE CHART

If my condition is **Reversible/Acceptable:**

Life-Threatening Illness	Cardiac Arrest	Feeding
Palliative		Basic
Limited	No CPR	Supplemental
Surgical	CPR	Intravenous
Intensive		Tube

If my condition is **Irreversible/Intolerable:**

Life-Threatening Illness	Cardiac Arrest	Feeding
Palliative		Basic
Limited	No CPR	Supplemental
Surgical	CPR	Intravenous
Intensive		Tube

_____

Date   Signature

_____

Power of Attorney Signature(s)

_____

Physician Signature

Date of next review should be once a year, after an illness, or if there is any change in health.

_____

Date   Signature

_____

Power of Attorney Signature(s)

_____

Physician Signature

4. DEFINITIONS

Reversible/acceptable condition: Condition where I have an acceptable quality of life

Irreversible condition: Condition where I have intolerable or unacceptable disability, for example, multiple sclerosis, stroke, severe head injury, Alzheimer's disease

Feeding

Basic feeding: Spoon feed with regular diet. Give all fluids by mouth that can be tolerated, but make no attempt to feed by special diets, intravenous fluids, or tubes.

Supplemental: Give supplements or special diets, for example, high calorie, fat, or protein supplements

Intravenous: Give nutrients (water, salt, carbohydrate, protein, and fat) by intravenous infusions

Tubes: Use tube feeding. There are two main types:
Nasogastric Tube: a soft plastic tube passed through the nose or mouth into the stomach
Gastrostomy Tube: a soft plastic tube passed directly into the stomach through the skin over the abdomen

Cardiac Arrest (CPR)

No CPR: Make no attempt to resuscitate.

CPR: Use cardiac massage with mouth-to-mouth breathing; may also include intravenous lines, electric shocks to the heart (defibrillators), tubes in throat to lungs (endotrachial tubes).

Palliative Care
- keep me warm, dry, and pain free
- do not transfer to hospital unless absolutely necessary
- only give measures that enhance comfort or minimize pain, e.g., morphine for pain
- intravenous line started only if it improves comfort, e.g., for dehydration
- no x-rays, blood tests, or antibiotics unless they are given to improve comfort

Limited Care (includes Palliative)
- may or may not transfer to hospital
- intravenous therapy may be appropriate
- antibiotics should be used sparingly
- a trial of appropriate drugs may be used
- no invasive procedures; e.g., surgery
- do not transfer to Intensive Care Unit

Surgical Care (includes Limited)
- transfer to acute-care hospital (where patient may be evaluated)
- emergency surgery if necessary
- do not admit to Intensive Care Unit
- do not ventilate (except during and after surgery); i.e., tube down throat and connected with machine

Intensive Care (includes Surgical)
- transfer to acute-care hospital without hesitation
- admit to Intensive Care Unit if necessary
- ventilate patient if necessary
- insert central line; i.e., main arteries for fluids when other veins collapse
- provide surgery, biopsies, all life-support systems, and transplant surgery
- do everything possible to maintain life

5. SIGNATURES

Family Physician

Name: _____

Address: _____

Tel: (H) _____ Tel: (W) _____

Signature: _____

Power(s) of Attorney/Substitute(s)/Proxy(s)

1. Name: _____

Address: _____

Tel: (H) _____ Tel: (W) _____

Mobile Tel: _____

Signature: _____

2. Name: _____

Address: _____

Tel: (H) _____ Tel: (W) _____

Mobile Tel: _____

Signature: _____

Witnesses

1. Name: _____

Address: _____

Tel: (H) _____ Tel: (W) _____

Signature: _____

2. Name: _____

Address: _____

Tel: (H) _____ Tel: (W) _____

Signature: _____

Guardianship

If a person becomes incompetent and has made no provisions, the courts will appoint a guardian on his or her behalf. The incapacitated person then becomes a ward of the court and a legal guardian is appointed. Guardianship is a much more expensive and cumbersome process than the durable power of attorney, and very few of us would want our families to go through this if it can be avoided.

The courts use guardianship to protect incompetent people who cannot manage their own affairs. Before a person is made a ward, he or she must be declared incapable. Once a legal judgment of incapability has been made, the ward loses the right to make decisions, including the right to make contracts, to marry, and to make his or her own health-care decisions.

The guardian is often a relative who applies to the court to become the ward's guardian. The decision is made in a hearing, which takes evidence of the person's incompetence and determines guardianship to be in his or her best interests. The person who applies to become guardian argues why he or she is qualified and the most suitable person to carry out the task. Once appointed, the guardian manages the ward's estate and finances and may make decisions for medical treatment, and so on. The guardian must file accounts with the courts on a regular basis and must obtain the courts' approval to carry out certain transactions, such as the sale of the ward's home if the ward is admitted to an institution.

Wills

This is the most widely used document for future planning. A will can be executed by anyone over the age of 18 who is considered to have testamentary capacity (is competent to understand the range of choices available and the implications of these choices). Anyone 18 or over who understands the purpose of the proceedings and who does not benefit from the will can act as witness to the will.

A will can be used for a variety of purposes: it directs who should receive particular pieces of property or possessions; it can give directions for burial or funeral rites; it can direct assets into a trust or to an attorney who will manage these assets for a child, or disabled parent, or other person. The will can be changed at any time, but a rule of thumb is that it should be written for a five-year span. At the end of five years, it can be completely rewritten or a codicil can be added. (A codicil is a document added after the fact to save rewriting the whole will.)

There is no such thing as a simple will and, if the will is not drawn properly, it can lead to lasting friction and dissension among family members. It is best to involve a lawyer. The lawyer ensures that the will truly represents a parent's wishes, that all eventualities have been accounted for, and that the will is an acceptable document. For example, it is important to make sure that, if one of the beneficiaries dies, alternative provision has been made for disposing of the bequest. An executor who will be able to manage the estate well should be appointed. Parents should discuss their wishes with this person in advance of drawing up the will.

Although a very important document, the will is usually only a part of estate planning. A will may not deal with joint bank accounts, real estate held jointly, or insurance policies. Joint accounts become the property of the surviving principal. Insurance policies are paid to the beneficiary therein named.

The will should be kept in a secure place, where it can be easily obtained. A secure place at home or in the attorney's office is recommended. A bank safety deposit box is not recommended as there may be problems gaining access to it after death, which can delay the probate of the will. Banks automatically seal the boxes after death. Wherever the will is kept, it is important to leave clear instructions, so it can be located easily.

Trusts

A trust is a means whereby a person (the grantor) transfers assets (corpus) into the name of another person or institution (trustee) to be handled as directed in the trust document. The trustee manages the assets for the beneficiaries of the trust. A trust can be created during your parents' lifetime or after their deaths through their wills. A revocable trust can be broken and the assets returned to a parent's name, while an "irrevocable" trust cannot be broken and the assets cannot be returned to a parent's name or estate.

A trust can be simple or complex; it depends on a parent's needs. Trusts are usually written by lawyers to meet a parent's specific needs and to ensure they are legal. Trusts need to be signed by the grantor to be valid. There is no involvement with the courts unless the trust is contested. Trusts can continue through succeeding generations and avoid probate proceedings.

Trusts are usually used to provide a caretaker for assets for minors or others who are considered unable to manage the assets on their own. Trusts can preserve assets for the grantor's purposes, in spite of later incompetence, and establish a trustee to manage them. They can be used to shift income tax to a person in a lower tax bracket or to pass property at death and avoid probates.

The cost is variable, depending on the complexity of the set-up. The trustee is entitled to a management fee. Trusts provide an effective way for older adults to acquire professional management of assets, avoiding the need for guardianship of those assets in the event of incompetence.

8
Keeping in Touch with Out-of-Town Parents

Children who live far away from parents and do not visit regularly behave differently toward their parents than do children who live close by and maintain regular contact. Children who live close by are usually better able to accept a parent's aging than are those who live out of town! One behaviour is so typical among the latter that I wrote it up in *The Journal of the American Geriatric Society* as "The Daughter from California Syndrome." This was the case.

Mrs. M., an 83-year-old widow with a five-year history of Alzheimer's disease, had been cared for by her 60-year-old daughter, who had never married and had taken early retirement to look after her mother. Mrs. M. had been admitted to a nursing home six months previously because she no longer recognized her daughter. She was incontinent and needed to be washed, dressed, and fed. In the nursing home she fell and broke her hip, which was surgically repaired in our hospital. Following surgery, she was unable to walk and required two people to lift her.

We discussed her care with her daughter, and she asked that if her mother developed pneumonia, we would not use antibiotics, and if her heart stopped, we would not attempt to get it going again. She wanted palliative care. The goal of treatment was to keep her mother comfortable but not to prolong her life.

One day I was in my office when the nurse from the floor called me. "Dr. Molloy, come quickly, Mrs. M.'s daughter is here and she is screaming and threatening the staff. She is insisting that we take Mrs. M. to the Intensive Care Unit immediately. She says she will sue us all for the negligent care we are giving her mother. She wants to speak to the surgeon and the administrator of the hospital. Please come, she's going crazy up here."

I was flabbergasted. "Are you sure you're talking about Mrs. M.? Her daughter Joan is so shy and gentle, you must be mistaken. We met with her..."

She cut me off. "Oh, no, Willie. This is not Joan. We haven't met this one before. This one is a virago. She just flew in from California."

The daughter from California was an angry, hysterical woman. We talked to her over the next week while she was visiting. Over the previous four years she had never come to visit her mother. Now she would never have a final conversation with her and she felt cheated. She kept saying that she wanted us to "bring her back," but it was too late. She never came to terms with the fact that her mother was dying. When she left after a week, there was an enormous collective sigh of relief from all the staff. We had spent hours with her trying to deal with her anger, guilt, and shame.

It's not unusual for the children who are farthest removed to have the greatest emotional reaction to a parent's death or illness. The children who are close by, in regular contact, see the gradual deterioration and are better able to accept the inevitable. Children who are removed and out of touch often react with shame and guilt. This can appear as a strong outburst of anger in which they project their feelings and blame others for the parent's illness or death.

When this guilt and anger is projected onto other family members, I call it the "How Could They Do This to Grandma?" syndrome.

John and Mabel are a middle-aged couple with two teenage children. Mabel's mother, Astrid, a widow, developed Alzheimer's and could no longer cope at home. Astrid lived in an apartment, had a few thousand dollars in the bank, and lived on a small pension. Mabel paid the bills, shopped, cooked, cleaned, and cared for Astrid.

Mabel's sister, Gwen, lived in another state and phoned on holidays and anniversaries. She came to visit every few years. When she heard that Astrid was moving into Mabel's house, she objected because she claimed that her sister was exaggerating their mother's problems.

Mabel cared for Astrid until it became obvious that Astrid needed to go to a nursing home. Mabel was exhausted and her family had had enough. When she told Gwen of the plan, Gwen objected and accused Mabel of making it up and dumping their mother in a nursing home. "How could you do this to Mom?" She swore that she would never speak to Mabel again. When Gwen came to visit her mother, she tried to get her transferred to a nursing home in her city, claiming that she would have taken her into her home if she had been given the opportunity.

I don't think Gwen will ever speak to Mabel again. The family was fractured, and Mabel and her side of the family were forever tarnished by the "How Could They Do This to Grandma?" syndrome. It's a destructive coping mechanism, but unfortunately not that uncommon. These two daughters had been in competition for years. One daughter used her dying mother to have a last shot at the other. It's not a great lesson for the next generation.

Conspiracy of Silence

Recently a friend called me for advice. His 84-year-old mother, visiting from Europe, had tripped and fallen. He wanted me to check her out. I did and she was fine. He had been living in the United States for thirty years and had married and raised a family. His mother came to visit every four or five years, and he went home about every other year. He felt guilty that she was getting older and more frail, and he was so far away. When he and his mother were in the office, I asked them what they were doing about the mother's problems when she went back. They had not discussed it.

I asked my friend how he felt. He had never spoken to his mother about what she expected from him. They had never discussed how they communicated with each other. He was feeling so guilty that he became very emotional and had problems even discussing the subject. He had problems accepting that she might need to leave her home and live in a retirement or nursing home. He was not ready. He said he would try to get home as often as possible and would do "everything" he could. He planned to go home to visit every year for a "week or two." He said he tried to write, but was a bad letter writer. He tried to remember to send cards and gifts but usually left it to the last minute, and felt guilty when his cards and letters arrived late. He felt very guilty that she was failing and he was not there to help, but she didn't want to move to the United States. He tried to phone weekly but often forgot.

I asked the mother how she wanted her son to communicate in the future. She said she liked him to phone every week to let her know what was happening. She wanted to know that he and his wife and children were okay. She worried about them being so far away. The weekly phone call was all she needed. I asked her about gifts at Christmas, birthdays, or anniversaries. She didn't want any. She didn't care for letters or postcards. She was financially stable. All she wanted was the weekly phone call. She didn't even want him to go to the bother of coming to visit for a week every year. She found the visits intense and exhausting. The flight was expensive, a week was a short time, and she knew it took him away from his family holidays. She said he was the best son a mother could have and felt he did more than enough for her. First and foremost, she didn't want to be a burden to him.

Her son was amazed that she cared only about the weekly phone call. He was relieved that she did not expect him to come home every year. He was shocked that she had already made arrangements to move to a retirement home. She had not told him because she didn't want to burden him.

Together they developed a communication plan, ground rules, and expectations. They agreed that he would phone every week. She didn't want his money or gifts. She told him that she was proud of him because he was such a kind and faithful husband and father. She wanted him to take care of his family first and foremost. She had made all her own arrangements to get more help if she needed it, and to move to a retirement home when the time came. He was very relieved. When they left the office, they were laughing about some of the phone calls, cards, and letters. His letters were so bad that they made her laugh. She pictured him sitting there trying to put words together—always saying the same things. They laughed in relief because they were resolving issues that had separated them and created anxiety for thirty years.

Most of the time we just have to talk to parents about their issues. It's amazing how simple the solutions can be. This single conversation lifted a burden that my friend had carried for half a lifetime. He finally got that particular monkey off his back.

Long-Distance Relationships

Communication with loved ones is difficult at the best of times, but when there are thousands of miles between us, it becomes even more complicated. Those who are separated from family and parents have to learn how to communicate in innovative ways. Although it takes extra effort to continue to communicate at a distance, it's well worth it. From a distance and a different perspective, one gains a deeper appreciation of family and parents, which can make relationships more precious and intimate. Living close by, family members often take one another for granted. Living at a distance forces one to become more creative and versatile. Adult children must learn to make contact by a wider variety of methods such as phone, letter, postcard, video, or audiotape. Communication can become more meaningful between people who live in different communities. For example, writing allows some people to express thoughts and feelings more easily. Meetings, when they do take place, tend to be more intense and satisfying.

Many people lose contact when they move apart. Others manage to maintain a meaningful relationship and grow even closer. How can the closeness be maintained? First, and foremost, make a commitment to keep in touch. Refuse to let distance and time come between you. Any contact is better than none for most parents and children. Each can derive comfort and satisfaction from the knowledge that the relationship survives in spite of the distance. There is a tremendous sense of achievement and satisfaction in finding new ways to express love and maintain bonds. One appreciates the effort the other is making, and this adds a whole new dimension to the relationship.

When parents know that their children have adopted their values and way of life, children offer parents a sense of immortality. Parents can always offer valuable advice, even to adult children, and children can also help their parents, despite being separated. Each acts as an independent outsider and can help to resolve family disputes and relationship problems. Distance confers a bird's-eye view and a certain neutral perspective, which can be valuable. In the time between visits or calls, there is time to think and digest the facts.

In telephone conversations, try to talk about what's important in your parents' lives. For example, if you phoned last time and your parents were getting ready to go on a small trip or preparing for a special event, remember to ask about it. This shows that you're interested in what's happening to them. If you hear a lot of complaints, just accept them and try "I'm sorry to hear you're not well. I wish I could do something to help. I hope it gets better soon and the doctors find out what's causing it. The last time I talked to you June was going for..." This way you acknowledge your parent's complaints. You empathize and acknowledge that you can't do much from a distance. Then change the subject to cheer him or her up. Sometimes it works. Sometimes you just have to listen to the complaints. It's important to make a parent feel that you will understand and offer a sympathetic ear.

Some parents find it hard to talk about issues that really matter in their lives, and talk only about ordinary, mundane subjects, like the weather. You may get off the phone and find you've talked about nothing at all. But that can be okay, too.

You Can't Put a Phone Call on the Fridge

Many people are complete failures at writing letters. There are some tricks that help to make up for this. Next time you're in a stationery shop, buy a variety of postcards or greeting cards for birthdays, Valentine's Day, Mother's Day, Father's Day, and other occasions, as well as some with funny messages. Keep an ample supply and buy lots of stamps. Send them off whenever you think of it. You can even write them all at once and just mail them when you remember. Everyone loves to receive a card in the mail. If you phone and one of your parents is not feeling well, mail a Get Well card from your supply. It's cheaper than a phone call and you can't hang a phone call on the fridge.

At the beginning of the year, mark your calendar with parents' birthdays, anniversaries, and special occasions. That way you'll remember to send cards in time.

Enclose a few photographs or children's paintings with the cards. Parents love to have up-to-date photos of children and grandchildren. When you're having film developed, always order a second set of prints.

Gifts

If parents request money rather than gifts, give it. Give telephone calls or a calling card so they can call you more often.

Every parent and grandparent wants a wallet-sized photo of children and grandchildren. Keep them up-to-date. A photograph album with pictures of your family is a great gift, or send large framed photos of yourself, spouse, children, and friends. My parents' home was covered with photos of our family. My brothers and sisters, who lived close by, didn't give photographs because their children visited more often.

If you're on vacation, send parents a postcard to let them know you're thinking of them.

It's nice to be able to communicate in different ways. One magical gift is a videocassette recorder (VCR) so you can send copies of your family videos. Most radios now have a tape deck attached and you can record your messages so they can play them back. You can also send them their favorite music or talking books.

Do they like to go out? Give season's tickets for sports or cultural events, a series of massages, a manicure, hairdo, or whatever you think they will like. There is never any need to give a scarf, a pair of socks, or a tie. Next time you're at home, pay the florist in advance for Mother's Day, birthdays, and anniversaries. You can cover a year or more in just one trip.

Get them an annual subscription to *National Geographic, Time, Gardener's Weekly*, or some other magazine that deals with an area they are interested in. I would not recommend a subscription to *Reader's Digest*, which generates cheap gifts, sweepstakes opportunities, and junk mail. Many elderly people find the *Reader's Digest* sweepstakes very misleading and confusing. Some continue to send subscription money because they believe they have won millions of dollars.

Keep on the lookout for books they might enjoy. Send mementoes, mugs, and placemats to let them know where you've been on business and holiday trips. Put your photo on a mug and mail it to them. Send calendars and fill in important dates so they will know where you are and where you will be. This can also serve to remind them of birthdays, anniversaries, holidays, and other important dates in your life. How about a bird-feeder?

Parents Visiting

The most important thing about any visit is to prepare in advance. A great deal depends on the parents. Some require little attention, while others want to spend all their time with you. If your parents fall into the second category, make sure you are on holidays when they visit or take time off work so you can give them enough attention. Plan to make the visit short and intense rather than long and drawn out. If your folks don't get along with your spouse, plan the visit when he or she is away. That way you can have more time together. Parents often resent others who take your time and attention when they're visiting.

Plan day outings, and have a backup plan ready if the weather is not accommodating. Contact any friends of your parents' vintage and arrange for them to meet. These friends can often give you advice about where to take your parents. Plan ahead, but try to leave the schedule flexible so they can decide what they would like to do. If possible, plan the visit around a birthday, anniversary, or other special occasion. This is a great excuse to have your friends over and make a fuss over your parents by throwing a party in their honour.

The last time my father came to visit, my wife threw a party for him just two days after he came. He met our friends and felt very honored that we went to so much trouble for him. We invited our older friends so he would be more comfortable. They invited him for lunch and dinner and to shows. He enjoyed going out alone with them. It was a welcome break for everybody. When I phoned after the visit, he always asked about these friends, so we had lots to talk about. He felt part of our circle of friends, and even communicated with some of them himself. This worked out very well.

Living at a distance from parents is bittersweet. It takes commitment to maintain contact, but, with a little effort and imagination, it is possible to do it.

9

Grief and Bereavement

After my mother's stroke in May 1993, she went to live in a nursing home. She needed to be washed, dressed, and fed every day. I phoned home regularly and spoke to my father and different family members. My sister told me they had a portable phone in the nursing home, so I got the number and called.

"Hello, is this Maypark Nursing Home? My name is Willie Molloy. I'm calling for Mary Molloy."

"Oh yes, we heard you would be calling."

"Yes."

"Well, she's just here—we were expecting your call. I'll put her on. She won't say much, but I think she will understand you. She is expecting it. So just talk to her—go ahead."

"Hello, Mum, hello."

I waited for an eternity, straining to hear every sound. Although I could hear her heavy, uneven breathing, there was no sound of a voice. The breathing was changing, but there was nothing else. I knew she was there. I could sense her expectation. I spoke again.

"This is Willie, Mum. I called to say hello. I called to say I love you and I miss you. I hope you are well. Can you say my name, Mum? Can you say 'Willie'?"

Again, I waited, growing more desperate. My father had told me that she had difficulty speaking, but I had expected her to say something. After a long silence, I spoke again. I wasn't sure if the phone had fallen, or if there was anyone there. I could faintly make out breathing.

"Hello, is that you, Mum? I can hear you breathing on that end. I love you very much. I'm sorry I didn't get home before this, but I've been very busy. I hope you understand. The children are getting so big—you won't even know them. I sent photographs. Did you get them?"

I waited . . . .

"It's Willie, Mum. Can you understand me? Hello, hello . . . I just want to tell you that I will always love you."

I started to break down. My voice started to break up and I was overcome by an intense feeling of emptiness, loss, and despair. I tried to speak, but only sobs came out.

Finally, the nurse picked up the phone and said, "Mr. Molloy, she's crying. Are you finished?"

"Yes, yes, I'm finished." I hung up, sobbing. I never tried to phone her again.

I finally went home in February of the next year. It was eight months after the stroke. I felt guilty for waiting so long. She was always in my mind. I think I was avoiding going home again because the last time I had been at home I knew that she was dying. When I was leaving I said to her, "I want to see you again. We will meet again." I made her promise that we would meet again.

My father and I went to see her on the Saturday evening I arrived. He told me it was too late to visit her because she would be tired, but I had to see her. I was so close that I couldn't bear not going that night.

The nursing home, an old Georgian house, was situated

high up above a bend in the river. The fields around it were lush with spring growth, and there were daffodils in the grass. The home itself was brightly painted and well kept. We walked through tall glass doors, and my father led me along a corridor, then stopped and pointed at a door. "She's in here. I come every day. Often I just sit and don't say anything. She won't speak now, she will be tired. So don't stay too long. I'm going for a walk on the riverbank. I'll come back and then we can go."

The room was enormous with tall ceilings and a large bay window overlooking a garden surrounded by thick laurel hedges. Darkness was creeping through the room. I could just make my mother out in the bed in the corner. She had changed drastically. Her face was shrunken, thin, and drawn. At first I thought she was asleep, but then she looked toward me with a puzzled expression. She was desperately trying to figure out who this stranger was. I held her hand and kissed her on the forehead, the skin so thin it felt like touching her skull. I spoke softly into her ear, "It's me, Willie. I'm home again. I'm sorry it took me so long." There was something very familiar that triggered a flood of memories, and tears welled up in my eyes, as I buried my face in her hair. She just looked at me with a puzzled expression.

My mother had been raised in Australia and had told us stories about Australia when we were children. She often wondered what kind of life she would have had if she had stayed there. I was the youngest of ten children; nine had lived. She had had a miscarriage before me. When she was pregnant with me, she had confessed to the priest that she did not want any more children. He told her that I would care for her in her old age and comfort her when she was dying. I always felt that I had betrayed her because I had not been around when she needed me.

That night I told her about Melbourne and my travels in Australia and Japan. I rattled on about the children and showed her photos. She did not speak. After a long time I noticed my father standing quietly at the end of the bed. She looked up and when she saw him, a single tear rolled slowly down her face. As she followed him with her eyes, I realized how much she loved him. He stood there crying, frozen in his grief. They still loved each other more than I had ever realized. At that moment, for the first time, I understood my parents' relationship.

All my life I had believed that they stayed together for the children. My mother complained about my father's drinking and they often argued. She had been an only girl and had been spoiled. He was the oldest of seven children, his father had died when he was seven, and he had taken care of his younger brothers and sisters. They had been incompatible—she wanted to be spoiled and told she was loved, but he didn't know how. They sat together by the fire for years and never spoke very much.

Toward the end, my mother became difficult and confused. My father was very patient. Now I could see their love was an unspoken bond. They were never very good at expressing it in words. Perhaps there are some things we can't say. Their love was there, frozen in the moment, in their sadness and tears. They looked at each other, crying together for the longest time.

He finally spoke to her in his macho, joking tone, the way he did when he was teasing. Sometimes it was the only way he could talk to her.

"Do you recognize him? Do you remember him? It's Willie."

She only had eyes for him. He turned to me.

"She doesn't know you. She's tired. Let's go. We will come back tomorrow, in the morning."

I kissed her tenderly. She just watched him. He stayed at the end of the bed. When he was leaving, he turned to her: "I'll bring him out in the morning. It's late now." There was no mention of love or affection. It was an empty farewell. He missed another opportunity for tenderness or compassion. Love's bitter mystery.

Come Quick, Your Mother's Dying

I visited every day. On Sunday she had said my name and talked a little. I was staying with my oldest sister, Mary. On Tuesday, she was at work, and I was alone in the house writing. I was going to visit Mum in the afternoon. The phone rang.

"Could I speak to Mary Molloy?"

"I'm sorry, she's not here."

"Who is this?"

"It's Willie Molloy."

"Who are you, her son?"

"No, I'm her brother."

"Are you the one just home?"

"Yes, could you tell me who you are?"

"I'm the matron in Maypark. I'm sorry, I'm sorry to tell you this, but your mother has taken a turn for the worse and she's dying."

My heart sunk: "I'm coming straight away."

I phoned Mary at work. She left immediately to pick me up. I frantically phoned all the family members.

"Can you drive, Willie? I don't think I can."

I jumped in the driver's seat and drove off.

"Which way? You have to tell me the way."

"Oh Jesus, let me drive, I can't sit here. I'll go crazy."

We changed. She drove wildly, swerving all over the road.

"Oh God, Mary, be careful or you'll kill us both."

It was about seven miles to the nursing home by a wide, straight road. It felt like we weren't moving at all. There was nothing to say, so I sat numbly staring out the window. Finally Mary spoke: "I have driven this road a million times but it has never taken so long before. Will we ever get there?"

We finally arrived and raced into Mum's room. It was obvious she was dying. There was a death rattle and she was gasping for breath because her lungs were heavy and full of fluid. She was terrified. I ran to her side and kissed her again and again. Her forehead was freezing cold and wet.

"Oh, Mam, oh, Mam, you know I have loved you more than anybody else in this world. You were the most wonderful mother I could have ever asked for. You gave me everything. Everything I've ever done or felt came from you. You sacrificed everything for your children. You gave everything to us. I can never thank you enough."

I choked up and couldn't speak any more. The family started to arrive. Mary was kissing her and whispering in her other ear.

"Mam, there's no reason to be frightened. You go to heaven first and we will be with you before long. Soon we'll all be together again. We will always love you and think of you. It's just like going for a trip on a ship. You are just pulling away from shore and we are here waving good-bye. Please don't be afraid. We are all here with you now."

Then Mary broke down and I started to speak again. "I'm going to miss you every day of my life. I will always carry you in my heart; as long as I live I will always love you. Thank you for giving me so much. I'm sorry I hurt you so much and said unkind things to you. I never meant them. I only wished I had been a better son to you. I'm sorry I left and went away. Do you forgive me?"

Then she opened her eyes and stopped gasping. The lids were so heavy. She stared at me for a long time. The eyes were watery and there was no expression. She was holding on.

"Oh, Mam, I hate to see you suffer so. Please don't fight for me any more. I'm okay. I will be fine. Don't worry about me. You have given me more than enough. You can leave me now. I will never forget you, I swear, as long as I live. Please let go, Mam. I love you...." I started to sob and could no longer speak.

Then my sister: "Don't hold on so. Don't be afraid. Let go, Mam. We're all here. God will be good to you. You worked hard for your family and did your best. God is kind. Give yourself up to him, Mam. Don't suffer so. You don't have to suffer for us any more now."

Her eyes rolled up in her head and she smiled. She turned her head and there was a hissing sound. Black material welled up and ran down both sides of her mouth. The hissing continued and we wiped away the liquid.

"She's gone. Oh God, she's gone," Mary wailed. More brothers and sisters were coming in gasping for breath. A nurse appeared and started to say the rosary and we all fell down beside the bed and sobbed verse after verse numbly.

"Hail Mary full of grace, the Lord is with thee. Blessed art thou among women and blessed is the fruit of thy womb, Jesus. Holy Mary, mother of God, pray for us sinners, now and at the hour of our death."

Now and at the hour of our death. Now and at the hour of our death. Now and at the hour of our death.... It repeated like an echo of a familiar arpeggio or nursery rhyme. There are only two moments in life, now and the hour of death. I had said this prayer a million times during my life and never understood it. Now I held onto it like a lifeline to keep control and my reason. All the children were kneeling, arms thrown over the bed, some crying, some mumbling, others just staring into space. Each of us was touching a different part of our mother's body.

A nurse came and took us to a waiting room. Tea, coffee, biscuits, and whiskey appeared, and we sat down and tried to figure out who was missing and who had not been told. Seven of the children were there. We sat quietly, struck silent by grief. My brother Frank spoke. "Well, she's gone now. This is the day we all grow up."

Nieces and nephews began to appear, and each of them had to be told and comforted. After a while the room began to close in. I got up to leave and my father followed. We walked slowly and deliberately along the riverbank. Although signs of spring were everywhere, the countryside seemed frozen, empty of any feeling, like a painting in a museum.

We walked for a long time, not saying anything, until my father finally stopped. "That's far enough. Do you think she has gone anywhere? Do you think there is anything out there?"

I laughed. "You'll probably find out sooner than me. But, I really don't think it matters. This is enough for me. If there is some place after, great. But just to be part of this life and to have known you and my mother is enough for me."

We walked back slowly. I wanted to hug him and tell him how thankful I was to have him as my father, but the moment passed.

My sister June was in hospital, and when my mother died she was under a general anesthetic having varicose veins stripped. We decided that four of us would go to tell her—my oldest brother, Dick, Sarah, and Mary, and I. In the hospital June was sitting up in bed, her leg heavily bandaged. She looked exhausted.

Dick spoke and as soon as she realized what he was trying to say her chin quivered, her eyes filled with tears, and an expression of great sorrow drained her face. She seemed to age ten years. Each of us in turn spoke to her, and little by little we all started to cry, words stuttering and breaking as we shared her grief.

That night there were prayers for my mother at the nursing home. I kissed her one more time and wished I could see into her eyes again. The funeral director covered her face and closed the coffin. She was taken to the church for a Mass for the dead.

The church was full of old people, kneeling, sitting, standing, praying quietly with their heads bowed. I had lived in Waterford until I was twenty-six, two hundred yards from this very church. I had passed these old people on the street every day, yet I never appreciated that they grieved the dead at all the funerals. They mourned another traveler who had finished her journey and passed over.

When the ceremony was over, there was a long line of people who came to share our grief. Each one of them, in hushed tones, took hold of my hand and said, "Sorry for your trouble." Cousins, neighbors, old school friends, and strangers came to me as in a dream, their familiar faces worn by the passage of time.

The next day my father and I went to show the gravedigger the cemetery plot. The dead lay all around, small stones the only testimony to their passing. We walked among the gravestones, my father pointing out the resting-places of our ancestors. The air was fresh, the hedges were blooming, there were fresh flowers on many of the graves. The gravedigger was an energetic, earnest man. When my father showed him where to dig he spat on his hands, rubbed them vigorously together, and declared respectfully, "I'll make a good one."

That afternoon I went for a walk on Tramore strand, a wide-open beach about three miles long. There was a southwesterly gale blowing. I thought about young children drowned in the summer and the shipwrecked sailors lost on the beach. I felt the people struggling in the water, gasping as the sea dragged them down. During the famine times they carried the bodies on wooden carts and buried them on a hillside overlooking the bay. I saw the bodies piled on the carts as they bumped and rattled over the stones on the beach. They were buried by strangers far from home. Did they pray for them and lay them gently to rest?

After the funeral Mass we rolled the coffin outside, and her six sons lifted it awkwardly into the hearse. Then we drove quietly and slowly to the churchyard outside the city. We passed people in the street who stopped and took off their hats, blessed themselves, and said a short prayer. On the highway, though, cars and vans rushed by, breaking up the procession. Many even passed the hearse, rushing somewhere, too busy to reflect or pay their respects.

In the graveyard the bell tolled twice. We carried the coffin to the plot and laid it beside the grave. As the priest prayed for her soul, I stood at the end of the grave, more alone than I have ever felt in my life. Then they took the cover off the grave and the gravedigger appeared with a companion. They gently and carefully lowered the coffin down. It made a scraping noise as it wobbled against the sides of the grave and disappeared into the dark window to eternity. I remembered then her kindness. She was the kindest person I have ever known.

The Emotional Maelstrom of Grief

Many people want to run away when they learn of a parent's death. They want to deny it. "There must be some mistake. This can't be happening." Along with the anger, depression, guilt, and confusion, the situation may feel intolerable.

Survivors can experience intense anger and may feel like striking out at someone or something. They blame others. Depression, guilt, or confusion may push emotions to hysteria and nonstop crying. Many keep saying, "If only I had..." or "I wish I had not..." Later a sense of detachment takes over, causing one to feel numb and emotionally drained. Grief is a feeling of separation or loss, accompanied by intense emotions. The death of a loved one is exhausting and overwhelming, in part because death is not an object that we can touch or feel. It's defined in negative terms—the absence of life, not being alive. It's a black hole, filled with suffering.

Sudden death can hurl you into a nightmare, an overwhelming sense of disbelief. Children who are thrown into this experience become exhausted physically and mentally, and may even feel they are losing their minds. But when a loved one dies at the end of a long and painful illness, you may feel an incongruous mixture of relief, loss, guilt, and anger. One minute you may be laughing, the next overcome with sadness. It's an emotional rollercoaster.

The feeling of loss of control from this brush with death and infinity can be intensely threatening. Death represents the passage from an organic to an inorganic state. Mourners are stunned, stopped in their tracks, confined to rituals to carry them through the motions of bidding farewell. We wonder: "Will we ever get through the grief?" It can be like wandering through a dark cave, looking for the pinpoint of light that will lead us back to our normal lives. Eventually, most survive and come through the experience, with a renewed sense of meaning and hope.

The Healing Process of Bereavement

Once there was a young woman who lost her mind because of the death of her child. She took the dead child in her arms and went from house to house begging the people to heal the child. She carried the child to Buddha. The Blessed One looked at her with sympathy and said, "To heal this child, I need some poppy seeds; go and beg four or five poppy seeds from some home where death has never entered."

So the demented woman went out and sought a house where death had never entered, but in vain. At last, she was obliged to return to Buddha. In his quiet presence, her mind cleared and she understood the meaning of his words. She took the body away and buried it.

THE TEACHINGS OF BUDDHA

There is no shortcut to working through grief. You must talk, cry, and remember, and think through, act out, and live your grief. This is the path to healing. Following this path is heavy going and takes a lot of energy. That's why it's called "working through." If you don't work out your emotions, they will remain bottled up and emerge later as anxiety, anger, depression, or lethargy. The grieving process can last a lifetime, but most people work through it in two or three years. So how do you do it?

First, accept that your parent really is dead. Until children can let go and say good-bye, they can't resume living again. Many, particularly men, are conditioned to believe that expressing emotion is a sign of weakness and are unable to express their emotions in public. However, pushing down emotions is a temporary solution. These intense feelings surface again later, often with greater intensity. Crying releases tension and pain, and is an important part of healing. Expressing emotions releases them and creates a bond with others who are suffering.

Second, it's important not to use drugs or alcohol in the mistaken belief that they soften or lessen the grieving experience. They just serve to separate you from your real feelings and interfere with bereavement and the resolution of this experience. It's more important to listen and deal with the emotions being expressed than to try to suppress them. Drugs and alcohol merely postpone, or, even worse, impede healing.

Third, remember that feeling guilt is normal. It's human to make mistakes. We all regret arguments, insults, or harsh words; unkept promises; words never spoken; gratitude never expressed; or feelings never communicated. However, we shouldn't spend the rest of our lives punishing ourselves. Children should forgive themselves for mistakes made, learn from their mistakes and resolve to change and improve their behavior in future. Acknowledge and accept these failures and move on. Don't use your energy to eat away at yourself, causing anguish and regret. Sometimes it helps to apologize to the dead parent, ask his or her forgiveness, and do something positive—plant a tree as a memorial or donate time or money to a charity. Learn from the experience and resolve not to make the same mistakes in your current relationships.

If we continue to punish ourselves, thinking "If only I had done this or that," we cannot move on. Some even come to believe that they caused the death or increased the person's suffering. They believe that they actually had control and are responsible for everything that happened. This is unrealistic and damaging. Resolving these feelings gives us the strength to carry on.

Finally, after the funeral, take one day at a time. Don't move away or make major lifestyle changes too soon after the death of a parent. It's not possible to run away from grief. Those who move away to escape lose their supports, and they often find that they are more alone and isolated.

Try to maintain or even increase social contacts with your siblings and the remaining parent. If someone asks you out for dinner or to a show, go. Don't lock yourself away from life. Isolation can make you feel worse. Friends to listen, understand, and support you at these times really help. Others who are grieving may provide the best support. We learn that we are not alone and that we are literally surrounded by millions of others who are working through exactly the same experience. This can provide great solace.

Eat a proper diet, get lots of rest, and look after yourself. It takes time to put your life back together again, but day by day, piece by piece, we do it somehow. We manage to move on and find we are better and stronger for it.

The Rituals Around Death

Since Neanderthal man, humans have buried their dead. Funerals and burial rituals serve a number of important functions. They allow those close to the person to acknowledge their passing and say good-bye. Each person is unique, and funerals allow the survivors to celebrate the deceased's life, to consider his or her gifts, strengths, and frailties.

Some claim they don't want a funeral—"What's the point? When you're dead, you're dead." They don't realize that funerals are for the living, not for the dead. Funeral rites are extremely important for the survivors. Children and friends come together to express and share their grief and work through their emotions. When parents say they don't want a funeral or want only family to attend, the children are obliged to follow their wishes. However, children have the right to grieve together with their friends, in any other way they wish.

In the past there were many elaborate and curious customs connected to funeral rites. Because there were no foolproof ways of certifying death, the traditional wake was held for twenty-four hours because of the fear that some people would be buried alive. As much noise as possible was made to try to "wake" the dead person. It was also customary to pinch the corpse to try and wake it up.

Traditional funeral rites have now been taken from the home and relocated to funeral parlors. Most families have a period of visiting before the funeral to allow the family to share the companionship and compassion of friends who share their grief. Visiting can be awkward for friends, but most make a heart-felt effort to comfort the deceased's relatives and close friends. This helps connect survivors to life and reality at a time when they often feel disconnected. Some families set up remembrance tables with photographs and memorabilia of various kinds.

Some older people read the obituary column in their local newspaper before anything else. People seem to emerge out of the mists of the past to pay their respects. Our ability to comfort each other at a time of death is one of our finest attributes. Most have been through it, and the words "I'm sorry for your loss. I share your sorrow and grief" can be extremely meaningful for the grievers.

The funeral acknowledges that death and life are connected. Most of the service is aimed at the family, to acknowledge their suffering and encourage them to accept the loss and move on. The service confirms that the person is dead, which is the first step in the healing process. Funerals also give mourners an opportunity to reflect on the meaning of life and death. Death is a brush with eternity, and a mystery which may challenge previously unquestioned beliefs. The funeral rites are so removed from ordinary life that we feel transported out of our everyday routine. Everything is slower, more deliberate, and carefully planned. Every ritual action and expression has meaning and significance. Mourners, in black, emit no energy, move slowly and deliberately, overwhelmed by exhaustion; they cling to each other for emotional and physical support. They are apart from the real world, trapped in a surreal, almost metaphysical ritual of saying good-bye to a parent.

Funerals give us a chance to review where we are on our own journey, look where we are going, and review the whole process. We are forced to ask the most difficult of all questions: what does life mean? We review our life and put it into the context of death. We have no choice but to consider this question at this time. Each death of a loved one brings it back again. We can never answer it completely to our satisfaction because there is no single answer.

The question about the meaning of life faced at a funeral is the same one posed in old age. It requires a search for meaning in the face of despair and nihilism. This struggle to find meaning and compassion to deal with tragedy gives humans nobility. Touching the stiff, cold corpse; gazing into an empty grave; and seeing the coffin lowered down offer the most paradoxically tangible evidence of our mortality and eternity. The grave, a wound in the earth, is the exit from this life, from organic to inorganic matter, to the unseen time. Life is over and gone forever. The black hole in the ground is the window to eternity.

The funeral provides hope for the future. When we have been devastated by loss, there is a unique opportunity to make a fresh start with renewed purpose and hope for the future. From despair we find hope, from sadness joy, as we seek to replace our lost loved one and renew and increase our love and connections with those who survive. Death leaves a hole but also an opportunity to reattach to life and others in a new, meaningful way.

Maintaining your emotional health after the death of a parent is difficult. First you must accept that death has occurred. One way to leave no doubt for both family and friends is to have an open casket. It helps people to accept the reality of death. No matter how many cosmetics have been used to dress up the body, it is clear that the person is dead. The body is like marble—cold and lifeless, the expression frozen. A simple touch is enough to confirm this. Seeing and touching give new meaning to the reality of death. Some say they want to remember the person as he or she was, but the person is not the same, and never will be again.

Children should be included in the funeral rituals whenever possible. It's best to avoid euphemisms like Granddad "is asleep" or "has gone away." They may be terrified to go to sleep or may wait for Granddad to return. It's impossible to hide death from children. They need to talk about it so that they won't develop irrational fears. Their questions should be answered openly and honestly. They should be encouraged, but not forced, to become involved in the funeral rites and mourning, and they should be allowed to see and touch the dead if they wish. With patience and time, they will come to develop an understanding of death.

Finding Yourself

Life is a journey of self-discovery. In their twenties, people travel; take drugs; meditate; join cults and communes; and turn to music, diets, and religion. In middle age they find themselves tied down by families, jobs, mortgages, and stress. Many rush through their lives so quickly that they have little time to spend with themselves. The day-to-day narrative of the mind is divorced from inner feelings because so much of life is spent postponing, transferring, and projecting. Life passes by while we are making plans. Booth Tarkington said, "They live upon their great theme

'When I get to be a man.' Being human, though boys, they considered their present state too commonplace to be dwelt upon. So when the old men gather they say 'When I was a boy.' It really is the land of nowadays we never discover."

Once we start to become aware of our feelings, we can start to gain insight and control. If we live our lives well and learn as we go, we gain wisdom. We start to understand what is real and important and disregard what is not. We start to accumulate experiences and make sense of the whole journey. It's hard in the middle of the day, when one is striving and laboring to put the day in perspective. In the evening, thoughts and memories can provide precious insight; this is a time to relax, to relive old memories, and to make sense of the experience. The ego, striving to cope and survive, separates us from the true nature of the universe around us. Spirituality puts us in contact with the universe and removes the illusion of separation. It prepares us to return to the universe after death. It allows us to connect with the inner voice, the true self.

We start to understand that nothing truly happens outside of self. Everything is within ourselves, and peace and happiness are created within. We can be at peace with ourselves in spite of the world around us. Victims react to the world, so that their state of mind is dependent on those around them. Survivors live now. The past is gone, the future is a myth, and there is only this moment. When the world's noise is ignored, we start to discover our true selves.

Much of life is wasted on triviality because it's easier to deal with and control. Life can be frittered away on meaningless details. It's easy to fly a kite. You pull the string and it flies and dances in the air. Love and death are harder. They are abstract and lack boundaries. But to ignore them is to damn existence to superficiality. The place with the wide crack through the reality of our everyday lives is the place where we want to look the least. That's where the answers lie, though. Death makes the widest crack through reality. Looking into it can be frightening and threatening. Considering old age and death can change goals, values, and beliefs.

After our mother died, my brother Dick said, "There is something I want to tell you. As you know I have always believed that there is a God. I go to Mass and take communion every morning, I sing in the choir and volunteer for the church. I consider myself a devout Catholic. I've been on pilgrimages to all the holy places. My faith was my anchor all my life. Six months ago, one day in my office, I heard a little voice from deep within. At first I looked around it was so real I thought there was someone in the room. It was like a voice on the radio but coming from inside me. I was very frightened. I thought I was going mad. It was the first time in my life I ever felt such a loss of control. It said, 'You know there's nothing out there. None of this has any meaning.'

"For the last six months I have battled for my sanity. I lay awake at night, I lost my appetite, nothing made me happy, nothing gave me joy. Everything I worked for and believed seemed useless. My family, my job, everything will just disappear if there is no eternal life. I lost my faith. I had no answer for the voice. The voice was my doubt, suppressed all these years. This is not a fear of death. In the police force in Rhodesia I faced death many times. I have no fear of dying or death. This was a different fear, fear of nothingness. I had to completely reevaluate my life. I had to try to find meaning in my life even if there is no heaven or eternal life.

"Finally I found some meaning. It's really simple—life is good, my family and my life have meaning on their own. Even if there is no heaven, I feel that life is worthwhile. Now my faith is not a crutch. I have considered the other possibility for the first time in my life and found meaning there too. I still practice my religion. I face my doubts and my greatest fears. A world without God is not necessarily a world without meaning. This realization completely changed my life.

"I am telling you this because I am sure that this will also happen to you. I am sixty now, getting ready for retirement, and am facing these issues. I am looking at old age and starting to reflect on my life and feel things I have never felt before. I keep changing all the time. You will know what I mean when you get here. It's okay. In many ways I am happier than I have ever been. Now I can't wait for my retirement. You will go through this. I want you to be ready. I will be happy to discuss it when it happens. All I could advise you now is to live every minute of your life with gratitude, honesty, and truth. Live your life, don't postpone it, don't waste any of it. Enjoy it all, the happy, the sad, don't shut yourself off from any of it. Love your family and friends. Then when you come to this, you will have no problems."

10
Toward a New Age

Throughout history, storytellers have mused about a cure for aging or places of eternal life. In Gaelic fairy stories there is a land called *Tir Na N-Og*—the land of forever young. In fairy land there is no time, no beginning or end. It is serene and quiet. Mortal life compared with this magical place is like a booby prize.

Heaven may provide immortality in the next life, but for those who want to avoid death, immortality here is their goal. More and more people are taking vitamins, herbs, lotions, creams, and treatments to prevent dementia and aging. Some treatments result from normal scientific inquiry, backed by clinical research. Others have more unorthodox origins. The Reverend Hanna Kroeger once described how she came to discover her cure for Alzheimer's disease. "'Jesus, help,' I murmured and here the heavens opened. 'Take equisetum concentrate, hawthorn, aloe vera gel.' I listened and that was the Lord's instruction." Reverend Kroeger believes that her treatment to unblock arteries in the brain will cure

Alzheimer's, although arterial blockage is not a feature of the disease.

Since there is no proven treatment or cure for memory loss and aging, many, believing that they have nothing to lose, will try anything. This exposes them to quacks and snake-oil salesmen. The increasing demand for cures for aging and for dementia means that some people may be encouraged to try drugs and other unproven treatments which are at best a waste of money, at worst a danger to health.

This does not mean that we cannot "do" anything for the aged. Adult children should have three goals for their parents. First, they should help their parents to adopt a healthy lifestyle to prevent and delay disability. Second, if a parent develops an illness or disability, children should do whatever they can to minimize the disability and maximize function and freedom. Finally, at the end of life, when a parent is dying, it is critical to ensure that technology and treatments are not used to postpone death and merely prolong the dying process. We can ensure that the elderly are treated with dignity, respect, and love.

Society mixes up illness with aging and considers aging as a disease. Many believe that all old people are sick, rigid, nonproductive, and grouchy. There are many active, happy, healthy 90-year-olds just as there are many sick, grouchy, rigid, and nonproductive people in their sixties, in their forties, or even in their teens. It is true that we are more likely to become ill and die as we age, but it is not inevitable that we will become chronically debilitated. Because of this confusion between aging and illness, many dread old age. They think they will automatically become ill as they age. As a result, they live in denial and fail to plan properly for what could be the best years of their lives.

Recently, a friend and I were leaving a chronic-care hospital when she said, "I dread the thought of growing old and existing on a bed with a feeding tube up my nose. I hate the thought of growing old and being like that." She was confusing old age with sickness.

In "On Old Age," Herman Hesse wrote that old age is a stage in our lives where each of us has something important and necessary to accomplish. Being old is an important, beautiful, and holy task. To fulfill the meaning of age and to perform its duty "one must be reconciled with old age and everything it brings with it. One must say yes to it. Without this yes, without submission to what nature demands of us, the worth and meaning of our days— whether we are old or young—are lost and we betray life."

The Aging Process

Everything changes,
Everything appears and disappears,
There is perfect tranquility
When one transcends both life and extinction.

SIDDHARTHA GUATAMA

What do a wrinkled face, a faded rose, and a crock of rancid butter have in common? Is it the same process that makes all living things grow old? If so, what is it, can we avoid it, can we stop it or at least slow it down? Would we want to?

Aging is so all-encompassing and complex that it is not easy to understand or appreciate. We can understand only particular aspects, like memory loss, changes in physiology, motor skills, sensation, learning, and communication. We are still seeking to identify a single unifying process that causes aging.

The body, made up of different organs, ages in its own way, at its own rate, so that different parts, in different sequence, slow down, wear out, and fail. The sequence and rate of aging in these organs determines the overall outcome for each person. Understanding how individual organs age and deteriorate is less complex than trying to understand how their aging affects the whole person. Developing a single theory of aging, or describing a universal process, as distinct from a description of the effects, is even more vexing.

Aging is a progressive, time-dependent loss in the ability to adapt to change. In the field of aging, the focus has shifted from attempts to understand how cells work and a description of cell function to a more fundamental examination and exploration of the underlying biochemical processes that determine the duration of life. Different theories attempt to describe a single universal aging mechanism to explain this process. Ultimately the search is on to find the key to unlock the secret of aging, to let the genie out of the bottle, to slow down the process, extend life, and cheat time.

Although there are many theories of aging, there is no single process that explains aging in all circumstances and conditions. It is likely that there are a variety of processes operating simultaneously to cause aging. Aging and death are inevitable in all normal cells. At the tissue level, cellular and molecular changes are caused by, or result from, aging. In most organs, age causes loss of cells and increasing irregularity of cell reproduction. This is a fairly universal phenomenon.

Each living cell that divides has a limited and predictable number of divisions. After a certain number of doublings, all normal cells stop dividing, and the cell dies. In this way, every living organism has built-in obsolescence and death. Leonard Hayflick found that normal human-embryo cells grown under the most favorable conditions experience death after about fifty doublings. The potential yield from fifty doublings of a single human cell is about twenty million tons. What changes this energy of life? Can it be prolonged, stretched, or even doubled? What is the spark, where is the control stick?

Cancer cells have broken free of these controlling mechanisms and are capable of infinite divisions. The chromosomes (long strands of genes) in cancer cells are different from those in normal cells, particularly at the ends. The end of the chromosome that may hold the coding to limit the amount of doublings is broken off.

The "Rate of Living Theory" suggests that there is a relationship between the total amount of energy expended and the life span for each species. Each organism has a limited amount of energy to expend, and once it is expended, the organism dies. If two members of the same species use up energy at different rates, the one that uses up energy faster dies sooner. This theory explains variations in some species' life span. For example, an insect's lifespan is proportional to the rate of its energy expenditure. Houseflies born in spring live about three weeks into the summer, while those born in autumn live six months longer because they are less active. Insects maintained at different temperatures live for different periods of time, depending on their ambient temperature. Water fleas kept at 27°F live almost 80 percent longer than those kept at 108°F. Those living at higher temperatures use up energy faster because they have higher metabolic rates. They have more than a 400 percent increase in heart rates. Over each lifetime, the number of heart beats is similar in both groups. Insects that can't fly live two and a half times longer than those that can.

This theory may explain differences in longevity in the same species. Within species, smaller animals live longer than bigger ones. For example, larger dogs don't live as long as smaller ones. Smaller body frames may last longer. It is also possible that smaller humans may have an advantage in longevity because they require less energy to live every day. This could even explain why Japanese live longer than Europeans; their smaller frames require less energy to maintain their metabolic processes.

Overweight people do not live as long as thin people. Animals and people who are at, or just above, the average body weight also live longer. Animals kept in captivity who are fed rations just below what they need to survive live 25 to 30 percent longer than animals who are given a free diet and are slightly overweight. Slightly underweight animals also have a marked delay in the onset of the diseases of aging. If we eat just enough to live, it seems we will live not only longer, but also delay many of the signs and diseases of aging.

So get up from the table slightly hungry, not stuffed and overfull. Eat a healthy diet of fresh vegetables and avoid too many fatty foods. A low-calorie, low-fat, high-roughage diet is key to health and longevity.

The Free-Radical Theory of Aging

Some claim that oxygen free radicals are responsible for making all living creatures grow old and die. Free radicals have been blamed for wrinkles, cataracts, thinning of bones, loss of flexibility, weakness, memory loss, cancer, and emphysema. Quite a list.

In the 1950s, Dr. Denham Harman first suggested that oxygen, the essential ingredient of life itself, could be the primary cause of aging, the gremlin in the machine. Oxygen is needed to extract energy from glucose to make energy and sustain life. However, the little oxygen molecule may actually contain a double-edged sword.

Negatively charged electrons orbit around the central part of the atom, the positively charged nucleus. Electrons spin in pairs to counterbalance each other. But the oxygen molecule is unstable because it has two loosely attached electrons in its outer orbit. It tends to take up or discharge electrons at a moment's notice. This leaves one electron short, and this element, a free radical, goes around grabbing other electrons to gain electrical balance. Free radicals live for just millionths of a second before combining with other electrons. They take electrons from molecules in the cell wall, DNA, or vital enzymes or proteins. This process is called "oxidation."

Oxidation by free radicals causes spoilage of fats, oils, and butter. It may cause almost 85 percent of the diseases of aging. When women with breast cancer have the DNA in their breast cancer cells examined, attached free radicals are present.

There is growing interest in antioxidants, chemicals that remove free radicals or enhance natural enzymes that do. More and more people take antioxidants in the belief that they slow the aging process. There is a wide variety of antioxidants available, ranging from vitamins to prescription drugs (see pages 240–242). However, when one considers that free radicals are made every time the body produces energy, last for millionths of a second, and cause damage in every organ throughout life, would it be possible to take enough antioxidants to mop them all up? One would have to almost continuous bathe every cell in these antioxidants to prevent oxidative damage. It hardly seems possible. Once again the solution to aging is a drug, a magic bullet, taken into the body. It frees the individual from taking charge of himself. It can be marketed and sold to a gullible public by modern snake-oil salesmen. It's easy, it feels good, it doesn't hurt. It's the perfect scam.

New and Improved

And modern humanity, upsetting all its idols, turned its eyes toward science, expecting it to vanquish suffering, old age, death. What a charming illusion, what a sweet dream to think of the freshness and the joys of the first twenty years of our life being added to the experience and wisdom of mature age!

J. BANDALINE, M.D.

Next time you visit a drugstore, take time to wander about and look at the products designed to keep you young and beautiful. On the cusp of the twenty-first century, image rules. The camera is more powerful than the gun or the pen, because we now see and learn in pictures. Appearance, or "charisma," counts most in a world where visual concepts are paramount and television debates determine who gets elected. We are bombarded by television commercials that "inform" us about which "look" is cool and which new and improved vitamin-supplemented shampoo makes hair shinier. The message is simple and clear: old is ugly, young is beautiful.

The media promote the common belief that the elderly are all the same—forgetful, rigid, and difficult to please. The names of successful elderly role models to counter this avalanche of negative stereotyping don't exactly roll off the tongue. Successful elders are perceived to be older people who look and act like younger adults. Seventy-year-olds who "don't look their age" and act like fifty-year-olds are praised. Never mind that this "achievement" was created by plastic surgery and cosmetics; it is somehow interpreted as having escaped the aging process.

This Hollywood beauty myth is both dangerous and destructive. We are encouraged to "fight" the aging process as we "fight" disease, and to view aging and its consequences as failure. In fact, aging is a natural process that is both normal and inevitable. How sad that so many are afraid or unable to look and act their age. They spend fortunes and precious time trying to mask the signs of aging. These misconceptions cause inappropriate expectations and generate negativity toward a completely natural and beautiful process. Children may actually reject their parents unless they can see through this negative stereotyping.

Although the term "golden years" suggests that old age should provide the most satisfying years of our lives, this time of life is often tarnished by the way it is portrayed by media. They can't seem to portray images of healthy, happy elders, especially women. They are obsessed with aging "problems" and offer a plethora of advice about diets, exercises, drugs, plastic surgery, creams, lotions, and vitamins to "fight" aging. Reference is made, again and again, to the burden of old age on the individual, family, and society. The elderly have been accused of creating an overly expensive "bedpan economy."

The level of denial and misinformation about aging in the media is staggering. A study of primetime television drama found that in 464 role portrayals, only 1.5 percent of the characters were over 65. Only 2 percent of television commercials contained older adults. From 265 newspaper articles on aging in the United States, *none* depicted older adults in a positive way; they all dealt with the *problems* of aging, such as reports of nursing-home abuse or retirees reminiscing about "the good old days." In popular magazines, the situation is worse. The elderly seldom appear in ads or articles about older adults. If they do, editors consistently include photos of the elders when they were younger.

This isn't surprising in a society that is adolescent in its collective pleasures and attitudes; that believes, if you don't look old, you're not old; that spends billions on products, creams, lotions, live-cell injects, herbs, and vitamins. This "perfect" advertised world would want us all to look like anorexic teenagers sitting in oxygen bars sipping carrot juice.

Since aging has been stereotyped as a predominantly negative experience, many older adults who develop such problems as weakness, arthritis, incontinence, or memory loss falsely believe that these problems are inevitable consequences of aging. As a result, they fail to report them and seek help. This attitude isn't confined to the general public. Older patients tell me again and again that, when they reported problems to their doctors, they were told, "Well, at your age, what do you expect?" Health in old age is a wonderful privilege, but the media haven't discovered it yet.

The Graying of Society

As the population ages, society stuck in adolescent denial is being challenged and forced to deal with the growing number of elderly. The most dramatic change in the twentieth century has been the doubling of the human life span. This will change society as never before. The huge age spread in families has produced gulfs between children and parents, even between children in the same family. This phenomenon is called the "generation gap." It was first used to describe the differences between teenagers and their adult parents.

Those who first experienced the generation gap in their teens are now faced with aging parents and, in some cases, grandparents. This new generation gap now constitutes North America's single greatest social challenge. Those in middle age are trying to grapple with the complex, often destructive feelings of anxiety, guilt, and confusion they feel toward their parents. Sandwiched between their parents and their children, they feel isolated and trapped. Parents, in their seventies and eighties, are struggling to deal with their old age in a rapidly evolving world which offers little security or predictability.

Children need to develop an understanding of the aging process to cope with these problems. Older parents and adult children have distinct needs because they live in very different emotional, psychological, and physical worlds. Misunderstandings arise when they fail to understand each other's feelings and behavior. Societies, worldwide, are beginning to grapple with the enormous impact that aging will have on resources, finances, social networks and supports, health-care systems, industries, and living standards in this new graying society. The greatest achievement of humankind is to provide a long and healthy life for its members. Old age is an achievement, the greatest gift a human can receive, not something to be endured like a curse at the end of the journey.

To cope with the issues presented by an aging society, we need to create a new world with drastically transformed systems, environments, expectations, and personal and public standards. We need to adapt and integrate our present models of health care and social assistance to cope with these demographic changes. There may be more than 2 million citizens aged 100 or more in North America in the middle of the twenty-first century. For every worker, there will be two older adults, and some have predicted that before the end of the next century the majority of the population could be aged 65 or more.

Innovative and creative solutions are needed to deal with the demands that aging places on our self, our families, and society as a whole. The first step is to educate ourselves and cope with our own parents.

"Cures" for Aging and Dementia

Western society values youth, beauty, efficiency, and vigor. Science, driven by this prevailing culture, views aging as a disease that needs to be "cured." Our rush to find a "cure" for aging and dementia, however, should be accompanied by an earnest discussion of the meaning, significance, and value of death and dying. The public demand for anti-aging and dementia treatments could ultimately lead to the development of treatments to slow the aging process. If a drug is developed that slows down aging, how will this affect society? By doubling the length of time an individual can live, will we double the suffering and the burden of illness on society? How could society function if 70 percent of the population was aged 85 or more?

As for the individual, will "treatments" for aging merely prolong frailty at the end of life, or add ten or twenty extra years of quality living? If we use fetal-transplant operations to treat dementia or prolong life, will this result in a worldwide black market for fetuses? Will the surgery be done in private clinics for the wealthy in countries where these procedures are poorly regulated? Will children in third-world countries be bought for their body parts? The related phenomenon of "smart drugs" has created an additional ethical dilemma: Are these the abuse substances of the future? Will businessmen who feel threatened by younger associates pop pills before important meetings to get an edge?

The benefits of new treatments will not come without costs. These costs will have to be assessed by public debate in the years to come. The public, researchers, and drug companies must develop an ethical framework to research and develop "treatment" for aging. Science and ethics can no longer be separate in this area.

The real challenge, then, is to come to terms with aging and mortality. This means that new developments in treatment need to parallel a new, realistic view of aging and an acceptance of death. In the face of an inevitable outcome such as death, the quality of dying should be as important as the quality of living. By blindly imposing our technological will on nature's course, we may act to its detriment. In this context, as new technologies evolve, we must question the fundamental value of these interventions not only for ourselves, but for society as a whole.

"The Man Who Did Not Wish to Die" by Shunsui Tamenaga (1790–1843) is the story of a Chinese emperor named Shin-no-Shiko, one of the most powerful rulers in Chinese history. He built many large palaces as well as The Great Wall. He had everything he could wish for, but he was miserable because he knew one day he would die and leave it all behind. He longed to find the "Elixir of Life." An old courtier named Jofuku said that, in a country named Horaizon (Mount Fuji), certain hermits possessed the secret "Elixir of Life." Whoever drank it lived for ever. The emperor ordered Jofuku to go to Horaizon and bring back the elixir. He reached the island and never returned. The hermits who lived there worshipped Jofuku as their patron god.

A man named Sentaro also wished to prolong his life. He sought out the hermits who lived on Mount Fuji. He prayed at Jofuku's shrine for seven days and seven nights. On the seventh night, Jofuku appeared. He advised Sentaro that the life of a hermit was too strict for him. Instead he sent him to the land of Perpetual Life, where death never comes and the people live for ever.

Jofuku gave Sentaro a little paper crane, and as soon as he touched it, it grew. He climbed on its back and it flew for thousands of miles until it landed on an island where there was perpetual life. In the memory of the islanders, nobody had ever died. Nobody knew what death was, but they all longed for it. They were all tired of their long lives. Sentaro was the only happy man on the island because he wanted to enjoy life for thousands of years.

Three hundred years passed and Sentaro also grew tired of living because life was always the same. He prayed to Jofuku to help him. The little crane popped out of his pocket and grew large. He climbed on its back, and the bird spread its wings and headed back to Japan. On the way, the crane dropped him in the ocean, where he was attacked by a large shark. As the shark opened its monstrous jaws to devour him, he screamed for Jofuku to help. Lo and behold, Sentaro was awakened by his own screams. He woke up before the shrine of Jofuku.

Suddenly a bright light came toward him, and in the light stood a messenger. The messenger told him to go back to his home and live a good and industrious life; never neglect to keep the anniversaries of his ancestors; make it a duty to provide for his children's future; and give up the vain desire to escape death. When selfish desires are granted, they do not bring happiness.

We should remember this story each time we hear about a new treatment or cure for the aging process. There is no treatment, demonstrated in proper studies, that slows the aging process or prevents memory loss. (These two conditions are considered together because of the close relationship between them.) The following have been touted as potential treatments.

Superoxide Dismutase and DHEA-S

Superoxide dismutase removes free radicals from cells. Animals who live longer have higher levels of this enzyme in their tissues than those who are more short-lived. It is not possible to take this enzyme orally because it is broken down in the digestive system and not properly absorbed.

Free radicals may slow down the secretion of hormones from major glands. For example, there may be a relationship between the levels of the hormone DHEA-S (dehydroepiandrosterone) and aging. Younger men have higher levels of DHEA-S than do older adults. Older men who have higher levels are less likely to suffer from heart disease, and have lower mortality rates. Women with higher levels of DHEA-S have less breast cancer and osteoporosis.

In January 1995, it was announced that clinical tests conducted in California showed DHEA-S produced a general feeling of well-being in patients who took small doses over a six-month period. Dr. Emile-Etienne Baulieu, inventor of the French abortion pill and the man behind DHEA-S, said: "DHEA-S won't make people live longer, but it will improve the quality of life over a longer period of time and will postpone some of the unpleasant effects of ageing such as fatigue and muscle weakness." He said that the compound would need at least two to three years of clinical tests before it could be manufactured for the general public.

The compound is secreted by the adrenal glands and shows up in the bloodstream around the age of 7. It peaks around age 25, and then starts to drop. By 70, most people have one-tenth of what they had when they were 25.

People who received DHEA-S said they slept better and had more energy. At this time, there is a shortage of proper studies which have examined the effects of antioxidants on aging and disease.

Vitamins

Almost half of North Americans now take vitamins or supplements of some sort. They have the most expensive urine on the planet. Vitamins are added to food, pop, shampoo, and creams. People take vitamins because they've been told they should by a billion-dollar industry that deemphasizes diet, exercise, and personal responsibility—it's easier to take a pill. The most popular vitamins are the antioxidants—vitamins C, E, and beta-carotene (vitamin A precursor).

Vitamin C is widely believed to prevent colds, cancer of the bowel, and cataracts, and to lower fat levels in the blood. Citrus fruits, berries, and green vegetables such as cabbage, Brussels sprouts, and broccoli are good sources of vitamin C. Vitamin C increases the absorption of iron and helps in wound healing. Smoking and stress increase vitamin C requirements. Recommended doses of supplements range from 100 to 500 milligrams daily.

Vitamin E may protect against heart disease by preventing the absorption of fats into blood-vessel walls. Whole grains and vegetable oils are a good source of vitamin E. There is a lot of work under way to examine the effects of vitamin E on heart disease, aging, and a variety of diseases. Vitamin E should not be taken by those who take anticoagulants (blood thinners) or have bleeding problems or vitamin deficiency. Recommended supplements range from 50 to 400 international units (IUs) daily. I recommend 300 to 500 IUs twice daily.

High intake of beta-carotene, a vitamin A precursor, is believed by some to protect against lung and throat cancer, heart disease, and stroke. Carrots, yellow squash, sweet potatoes, peaches, orange vegetables, and fruit are good sources. Beta-carotene, not vitamin A, is an antioxidant. They are often combined, so it's important to check preparations. Overconsumption of vitamin A can cause serious side effects. Consult your doctor before you take these vitamins.

Vitamin D increases calcium absorption. The body, with the aid of sunlight, makes vitamin D in the skin. Vitamin D is also found in cod-liver oil, butter, egg yolk, and liver. Too much vitamin D causes calcium deposits in the blood vessels, may raise cholesterol levels, and increases the risk of heart attacks.

B vitamins are called the "nerve" vitamins because they are believed to calm anxiety and lift spirits. For example, vitamin B6 is used in the treatment of pre-menstrual syndrome (PMS). B12 deficiency, which can damage the blood cells and lead to nerve damage, is common in the elderly. Vitamin B12 is usually taken by injection because a deficiency of acid in the stomach prevents its absorption from the bowel.

Recently a large trial of 29,000 male smokers in Finland, treated with vitamin E, beta-carotene, and placebo, found almost a 20 percent increase in lung cancer in those who received beta-carotene. The investigators concluded there was no reduction in the incidence of lung cancer after five to eight years of dietary supplements with vitamins E and A. The researchers were concerned that the vitamins may have had harmful effects and that the beta-carotene may have actually increased the risk of cancer. Again there is little reliable data to show that vitamins added to a balanced diet improve health or lengthen life.

Testosterone

The world was shocked when Canadian track star Ben Johnson tested positive for the steroid testosterone after he won a gold medal in the 100-meter Olympic final. He was later deprived of his medal and suspended from competition. The Dubin Inquiry into the use of performance-enhancing drugs in sports shocked the world by revealing that the use of hormones containing testosterone was almost routine in the upper ranks of professional athletics.

Testosterone, the male hormone, is responsible for male characteristics such as facial hair, large muscles, and strong bones. If it helps athletes win races, can it help older adults? Scientists are now starting to study the effects of testosterone replacement on frailty in healthy elderly men. With aging, some men experience a drop in the levels of testosterone. The drop may be partly responsible for a reduction in bone density, muscle mass, and muscle strength, and for increases in body fat seen in some elderly men. Investigators are focusing on males with lower testosterone levels to see if replacing the hormone will increase their levels in the blood and slow aging in muscle, bone, and brain. Some studies have reported that testosterone replacement in older men increased testosterone to "above the upper limit of normal" with a corresponding improvement in memory and muscle strength.

Study of testosterone replacement to slow or prevent aging is still in its infancy. Although this hormone has the potential to improve certain functions related to aging in some older men, its efficacy still remains unproven. The preliminary evidence is promising but not conclusive.

Falling levels of other hormones, such as growth hormone, may also contribute to frailty. Some studies are examining the effects of replacing both of these hormones at the same time. In animal experiments, growth hormone combined with testosterone raised serum testosterone levels more than testosterone replacement alone. Ongoing studies are assessing the effects of replacing a combination of hormones on strength, balance, memory, mood, sleep, and sexuality.

It's not clear if certain hormone replacements cause more harm than good. Testosterone is not a benign drug. It makes the prostate gland grow larger, increases the risk of prostate cancer, disturbs sleep, damages the liver, negatively affects blood production, and increases the levels of cholesterol and fat in the blood. More study is needed to determine who derives the greatest benefits, whether the benefits outweigh the risks, how it is best given, and in what doses.

Testosterone cannot be recommended for normal males with normal levels of testosterone in the blood, but it holds promise to slow the ageing process in some men.

Gerovital-H3 and H7

Gerovital-H3 has been strongly promoted for more than thirty years as a treatment to delay aging. It contains procaine hydrochloric acid, an anesthetic used by dentists. An anti-aging effect was originally reported by Ana Aslan in Hungary, who found that older people who received this supplement lived longer. Some claim that the older people fared better, not because of this compound, but because others were taking more interest in them. Their diet also improved and they exercised more. Gerovital-H7, a new version, is now being promoted by the same pharmaceutical company. Neither compound has ever been shown to have any beneficial effects in proper trials conducted by the scientific community.

Removal of the Pituitary Gland

This surgery has been used in an attempt to prolong the life span. It was done in the belief that there is a "death hormone" produced by the pituitary. Animals who underwent this procedure lived longer, but they also lost weight. Most of the apparent beneficial results may have derived from the weight loss.

Cell Therapy

With this form of therapy, live cells taken from animal fetus or placenta are injected into humans in the hope that substances in the young animal cells will invigorate older humans. This is practiced in clinics in Europe, and illegally in the United States. This treatment, unlike many others used to prevent aging, may be quite dangerous. The body may have severe reactions to these foreign cells. Cell therapy is completely unproven.

Chelation Therapy

Certain environmental toxins may contribute to aging and the development of Alzheimer's disease. Exposure to aluminum has been associated with the formation of senile plaques in the brain, a characteristic feature of Alzheimer's. Some have suggested a tentative relationship between Alzheimer's and the use of aluminum-containing pots and antiperspirants, and high aluminum concentrations in drinking water. Fluoridation of water appears to protect against Alzheimer's. Deficiencies of minerals such as zinc have also been implicated in the development and progression of the disease.

Chelating agents, such as desferrioxamine and bind aluminum, mitigate the damaging effects of environmental toxins on the nervous system. Desferrioxamine cannot be given by mouth; it must be injected. One trial, which used intramuscular desferrioxamine, showed a significant reduction in the decline in memory and daily living skills in the Alzheimer's patients who received the treatment compared with those who did not receive it. There were almost 800 percent more deaths in the group that did not receive des-ferrioxamine. However, the design of the study was not double blind, and many do not believe the results, which are very controversial.

Chelation is widely advertised to the public and is being used by an estimated 1,500 practitioners or clinics in the United States to treat senility and aging as well as a wide variety of ailments. Chelation is an unproven, costly, and potentially dangerous treatment in the prevention of aging. It also remains unproven in the treatment of Alzheimer's.

Nerve Growth Factors

One exciting area of current research is in programmed cell death, or apoptosis. In the embryo, cells are produced in excess and compete for the protein called "nerve growth factor" (NGF) which causes nerve cells to grow. Cells with the strongest response to NGF survive; the remainder die. But in some cases, cell death may be caused by genes. For example, as the fetus grows rapidly and changes, old cells are constantly being replaced by new cells. Cells that are replaced are programmed to die after they have performed their function. In a round-worm, *C. elegans*, two genes have been identified which prevent cells from dying. More recently a compound, bcl-2, was isolated in a B-cell leukemia and found to prevent programmed cell death.

This effect may be basic to all animal cells. The use of bcl-2 and other genetic mediators of cell death is now being investigated. It is not available for testing in humans yet. Since cancer cells seem to be immortal—they just continue to divide and divide—the chemicals which create these conditions may also alter normal cells and stop them from dying or growing old. These chemicals offer exciting new prospects to slow aging and treat Alzheimer's.

Nerve growth factors are unable to cross the blood–brain barrier, so cannot be taken by mouth or by injection. The blood–brain barrier acts like a filter to keep unwanted chemicals away from the brain. Instead, they must be implanted directly into the brain. Implanting nerve growth factor into the brain may rescue dying nerve cells. This may prove to be a very productive area of research in years to come as attempts are made to transplant nerve growth factors into the aging brain. Transplanted embryonic nerves may protect aging cells from decay by providing essential chemicals and growth factors. Already, aged rats have shown improvement after transplantation of embryonic nerve tissue.

Deprenyl

Deprenyl and similar compounds have been touted as anti-aging treatments. Some people are foolishly giving deprenyl to teenagers and pets in the belief that it slows the aging process. There are two MAO (monoamine oxidase) enzymes, A and B, in the brain. Deprenyl blocks the MAO enzyme B system. Other inhibitors, such as moclobemide and brofaromine, are short-acting, reversible inhibitors of the brain enzyme MAO. Moclobemide is a very powerful and useful antidepressant, now licensed all over the world for the treatment of depression, but it is not a proven anti-aging treatment.

The possible success of L-deprenyl in slowing the progress of Parkinson's disease is controversial and has led to speculation that it might benefit people with other diseases, such as Alzheimer's. The results of one recent fifteen-month double-blind study on thirty-nine people with Alzheimer's found no significant positive effects. L-deprenyl did not have a significant impact on behavior or memory, and did not appear to slow the progression of the disease. Further studies are ongoing, but have been disappointing to date.

Cerebral Vasodilators

Cerebral vasodilators, such as papaverine, betahistine, and nimidopine, act as smooth-muscle relaxants, adrenergic agonists, or selective calcium channel-blockers to dilate blood vessels in the brain. They have not been shown to have any effect on memory or aging.

Cerebral Metabolic Enhancers (CMEs)

Compounds like dihydroergotoxine and nafronyl improve carbohydrate metabolism in the brain. They are as yet unproven in preventing aging or improving dementia.

Nootropics

This is a very interesting new class of compounds which generally activate the brain in a fairly nonspecific fashion. Nootropics, such as piracetam, oxiracetam, CGS 5649B, and acetylcarnitine, selectively enhance higher integrative cerebral functions. They have very marked beneficial effects on memory in animals. Although they improve memory in humans, too, the changes are small. I have tested oxiracetam and 5649B in clinical trials. They have some mild beneficial effects and are remarkably free of any toxicity. It is almost certain they help some people more than others. Our challenge is to predict whom they will help. Newer, more powerful "next generation" compounds continue to be developed and tested.

Cholinergic Drugs

A wide variety of cholinergic agents, such as pyridostigmine, physostigmine, and tetrahydroaminoacridine (THA or tacrine), increase neurotransmission (nerve message-sending) and may improve memory in Alzheimer's patients. Cholinergic drugs, or anticholinesterases, block the enzyme cholinesterase. This enzyme breaks down acetylcholine, a chemical which carries messages between nerve cells.

THA is the first drug licensed by the U.S. Federal Drug Administration for treatment of Alzheimer's. It is interesting to note that it has not been approved for use in Great Britain or in Canada. The results and significance of the test results are still controversial.

Donepezil is a new and improved brain cholinesterase inhibitor that improves memory and function and avoids the side effects of THA (tacrine). Donepezil limits itself to the brain's cholingeric system and so does not cause side effects such as abdominal cramps, diarrhea, or liver toxicity. The dose that most improves memory and function is not limited by side effects. It is expected that this drug will be licensed soon in the treatment of Alzheimer's disease. It is not a cure—it simply improves memory and function.

Angiotensin-Converting Enzyme (ACE) Inhibitors

Angiotensin-converting enzyme inhibitors, such as captopril, inhibit the enzyme angiotensin and improve cognition and memory. They are licensed as treatments for high blood pressure. When they were used to treat high blood pressure, it was noted that some people who were treated with them had a significant improvement in mood and quality of life. In this way it was discovered by accident that they might have effects directly on the brain, independent of their blood-pressure-lowering effects. They are presently undergoing testing as potential treatments for dementia.

Smart Drugs and Smart Foods

Several drug treatments for dementia have been referred to in the lay press as "smart drugs." Certain faddists have proposed that the consumption of these so-called smart drugs in conjunction with "smart foods" can improve memory, even in those with no obvious memory problems. More than 150 "brain drugs" are being tested worldwide, and cognitive enhancement has become the tenth-largest area of pharmaceutical research. This research has the potential to benefit not only those with dementia, but also the general public. Smart drugs are designed to increase brain power through enhanced production of neurotransmitters in the brain. These compounds may have a positive effect only if a person is deficient—it remains to be seen if they have any beneficial effects on those with normal neurotransmitter levels and activity.

Little clinical research has been done to show that smart drugs are effective. Furthermore, many of the compounds promoted as "smart" such as piracetam, oxiracetam, and hydergine are no better than placebos. Piracetam, for example, is dispensed from bubble-gum machines in Italian hospitals. Catalogues are available giving information on how to order smart drugs, and one recent book, *Smart Drugs and Nutrients* by John Morgenthaler and Ward Dean, sold more than 75,000 copies in the first year of publication. Thus, despite the lack of any substantive evidence, people seek out and take these drugs at no small cost, hoping to achieve an intellectual edge in the ongoing search for the elixir of youth.

Smart drugs have fostered a new subculture where "smart" devotees frequent bars, restaurants, and parties ("raves") where "smart cocktails" and "smart foods" are served. In oxygen bars, clients sip vitamin supplements while wearing cannulae up their noses and convince themselves they feel good. Many have simply switched addictions from one form of drug-taking to another. Support for smart drugs often comes from former users of cocaine, Ecstasy, and mescaline. Although the reported benefits may result largely from a placebo effect, members of the drug-using subculture could possibly benefit if prior drug use had depleted their supply of neurotransmitters. Smart drugs like amino acids, tyrosine, and phenylalanine could potentially improve brain function by restoring these neurotransmitters.

Smart foods include a variety of vitamins, minerals, and herbal remedies. Again, apart from personal testimonials, no objective evidence is available to substantiate their effects. To date, smart foods and smart drugs have been used primarily by a small drug-using subculture and they have not been demonstrated to be of any benefit in improving memory or cognition in normal people or those with dementia in proper scientific trials.

Fear of Death

Survival is our strongest instinct. Death is our greatest fear. In the twentieth century this death phobia has driven the development of medical technology to such a pitch that the costs threaten to bankrupt every developed country. We spend billions prolonging life long after it has lost its meaning. We have developed religion, miracles, and heaven as crutches against an outcome which we cannot control or comprehend.

The thought that this existence is all there is, that we are an accident of creation, is too bare, too harsh, too cold. Is religion a delusion shared by billions to soothe our fears? Is it our collective coping mechanism? Is it the greatest deception of humankind, necessary to deal with our fear of extinction, to make sense of the unthinkable? Is God the panacea for our fears of death, infinity, and meaninglessness? Is God our comforter, our elixir of eternal life, his priests handing out hope like doctors prescribe sleeping pills to insomniacs? And if God does exist, how will he deal with us?

My parents' deaths pressed these questions on me. It seems the more I thought about their deaths, the more I realized that the only thing we can be sure of is now. So many sacrifice their lives in the hope that they will be rewarded in the great lottery in the sky. They use their energy in this life building up stock for the next. They have transferred their attachment from life to heaven and salvation. They spend their precious time praying to statues and images, and ignore the living. Still others kill because they call the creator by different names or believe that they have the only franchise to heaven.

My parents' deaths shattered my childhood fantasies. Life was not a fairy tale any more, with death in the far distance. The God of my childhood died. Like my brother, I had to consider the possibility that there is no God and come to terms with this possibility. Otherwise, religion would always be a crutch, a shield from the possibility of extinction. Society shielded from death by traditional religions is starting to contemplate death in a different way as more and more relinquish traditional religion to seek out a new spirituality. But before I could do this, I had to come to terms with time.

Coming to terms with aging means coming to terms with time. Time is a fire that burns everything to ashes. Like infinity, time is a concept that we cannot fully grasp or appreciate. It's hard to appreciate time outside of our own life, particularly before we existed or after we cease to exist. We can measure it in millions of years or in billionths of a second. This gives us a false sense of control and mastery over it. A wristwatch is like a statue of a deity or a crucifix around the neck. Yet we can't touch time or hold it, we can't store it or keep it. We are defined, mesmerized, and puzzled by time as it ticks on inexorably, relentlessly, eroding away our lives. The precious time we have provides the opportunity to enjoy, love, and appreciate life. We need to come to terms with and accept it, as it signifies mortality, extinction, and infinity. Time, before or after this moment, is meaningless. Life is now.

I had to stop dreading the future and trying to hold onto the past. When we think about our parents, we may feel sadness that they are becoming frail and will die before us. But that's life. We didn't make the rules. We can't change it. If we don't accept this, we can't get beyond these feelings. We will never be free to enjoy our parents without projecting our own anger, guilt, anxiety, and helplessness into the relationship. Stop trying to hold onto life like a lifeline to prevent you from sinking into the void. Live in the moment, take more chances, and try to master life rather than be mastered by it. But most of all, enjoy it.

Anything that causes anxiety, regret, or sorrow steals your time away. Striving for money, power, or recognition takes away from what you are now. Victims wish that life was different or that their parents could change. They reject themselves and their parents, and this causes regret and anxiety. It acts like a wedge between parents and children. Victims do not understand the difference between attachment and love. They are so attached that they are not free to love. Unless they deal with their attachments and relationships and their feeling toward them, money, power, and possessions will not fill these needs, close the void, ease their nagging doubts, or calm the heebie-jeebies in the middle of the night. Survivors, on the other hand, accept the conditions of life. They live unentangled by anger, denial, guilt, and dread. They are free to live.

A New Society

Society is slowly, reluctantly moving toward an understanding of aging, disability, death, and bereavement. There is no turning from the reality that life ends in death. Time and aging are natural, universal laws, and conditions of life. Understanding and coming to terms with them is a challenge we all face.

Each generation has a different experience. Baby boomers, who embraced political activism, health food, careers, and fitness, are now finding that meditation, tofu, jogging, and plastic surgery will not keep them young. Some are connecting with the cosmos in a different, eclectic way. They are beginning to experience, firsthand, their own mortality, and they are turning to a New Age spirituality that attempts to integrate philosophy, science, and religion.

Some are also coping with aging parents in unique and creative ways. Adult children at the end of the twentieth century are forging a new moral code to deal with an aging population. They are trying to develop a flexible relationship with parents and trying to maintain an ongoing dialogue.

Aging, suffering, and love, our greatest spiritual teachers, can open windows to a new understanding and appreciation of life. Coming to terms with our own mortality brings profound changes in our understanding and appreciation of our existence. It can change forever how we feel, act, and live in this world.

Happiness lies in the way we live every day. No matter what we wish for, or what changes we make, we cannot avoid suffering, disease, old age, and death. Wishing for anything else increases striving that traps and enslaves us. Most of us wish for longer lives. The problem is that once we were granted our wish, we probably wouldn't know what to do with the extra years. We have to learn to live and make the most of the time we have. Some people who want twenty more years of life don't know what to do on a rainy Sunday afternoon. Old age, more than anything else, offers us the opportunity to create the person we want to become.

The Old Joker

In general there are two types of old people—the "wise" know-it-all and the old joker.

Old jokers have accepted their mental and physical deterioration, illness, death, and dying, and are closer to wisdom than we might at first realize. They have rejected power and responsibility as well as the more traditional views of wisdom. Old jesters take up hobbies and causes. They work, not to drive the economy or maintain power, but to enjoy themselves and use their talents as they wish. Jesters act silly to amuse the grandchildren, take nothing seriously, and spoil themselves. Their children should appreciate the importance of this role and allow them freedom to play it.

Adolf Guggenbuhl-Craig, a Swiss writer, wrote, "When one accepts the folly of old age and rejects the projection of wisdom onto it, one has become fully individuated." The old fool or joker rejects being regarded as wise or intelligent. "Growing old becomes rewarding again. In old age we can rid ourselves of our power but also of responsibility.... There may be something to the saying that 'Children and fools speak the truth.'"

On the other hand, there is the "wise" old person who has fallen victim to the popular mythology and believes that wisdom brings knowledge and power. This old person tries to hold onto power, to control all decisions. These old know-it-alls become vain, righteous tyrants who are rigid and critical. They cannot tolerate any criticism and refuse to accept advice. Unlike the old fool who has given up control and begun to contemplate the great chasm ahead, the know-it-all tries to maintain control.

Like Narcissus, who looked into the water and fell in love with himself, the arrogant old person holds onto an image. The old jester, however, looks into the mirror, sees through the eyes and beyond. The jester has let go, has accepted his or her fate, and is getting ready to merge into the ongoing community of beings, past, present, and future, both living and nonliving. The jester challenges us to reconsider the meaning of wisdom.

The best thing about old age is that we can construct the person we want to become. We create our own persona in old age. The old joker sits in the cracks in the veil of reality. We can try to hold onto power and maintain control, victims bound by the past, afraid to move on. Or we can be one of the survivors who look through the cracks to infinity and beyond and smile at the great bittersweet mystery of this existence. Unlike any other phase in the life cycle, old age demands these choices—to remain attached, or disengage and move beyond this reality. It's your choice when your time comes.

Epilogue

In early January 1996, my brother Jim, a doctor in Waterford, Ireland, called me early in the morning. He had never phoned me since I left Ireland. I think he never forgave me for leaving.

"Willie, Dad was admitted to hospital yesterday with jaundice. He has cancer in his pancreas, which has spread to his liver. He doesn't have long."

I felt that sick, sinking feeling.

"I'm coming home."

He replied, "Take your time, we will try to bypass it and buy him some time."

I flew home and was in the St. James Hospital in Dublin when my father woke up from the anesthetic. They had successfully bypassed the blockage. Over the next week his jaundice faded, but he never regained his appetite. He was too weak to get out of bed. He had given up.

I went to see him every day in a six-bed public ward. There was no privacy and we talked about the weather, horses, the children, and the family. There were no profound words of advice, no acknowledgment that he was dying or that I would be leaving him and might never see him again.

On Friday I went to see him. I was getting the train to Dublin, starting my return journey home. We knew it was our last meeting. I sat there awkwardly and we both cried quietly. Eventually, it was time to go. I got up, we kissed, and I left.

A week later Jim called again.

"Willie, he died last night."

I immediately replied, "I'm coming."

"But you don't have to."

"I have to."

I got there in time for the removal. He had the biggest smile I had ever seen. The priest said the rosary. We went to the church. It was packed with the same relatives and family friends. They all said the same thing. "You're back again.... Sorry for your trouble.... But you know, he enjoyed his life."

"He enjoyed his life...he enjoyed his life." I realized the greatest gift he had given me was not to take life too seriously. He showed me how to laugh and enjoy life.

The day of the funeral was a typical Irish spring day, all four seasons at once. It rained and the sun was shining at the same time.

They lowered him into the grave. I looked up—there was a rainbow. I nudged my brother Frank. He smiled "There's Jem [my father] for you—laughing at us all." The wind rustled the trees. It was my mother in the softness of its breath, it was my father as real to me as the covenant of hope displayed in the rainbow. Mother wind, Father rainbow.

Index